TAQWA AND KNOWLEDGE

TAQWA AND KNOWLEDGE

A TRANSLATION OF
A DISCOURSE ON TAQWA AND
A DISCOURSE ON KNOWLEDGE
FROM
AL-NASÂIH AL-DÎNIYYAH

Imâm al-Haddâd

KITABA

Publisher: Kitaba – Islamic Texts for the Blind, Glasgow, UK

Email: info@kitaba.org

Website: www.kitaba.org

Title: Taqwa and Knowledge

Author: Imâm al-Haddâd

Translator: Abdul Aziz Ahmed

Typesetting: Abdassamad Clarke

ISBN: 978-0-9559649-3-0

Printed by: MPG Biddles Ltd.

                    www.biddles.co.uk

                    Tel: 01553 764728

Cover design by: Que Media, Info@quemedia.co.uk

CONTENTS

بسم الله الرحمن الرحيم

In the name of Allah
Most Gracious
Most Merciful

ACKNOWLEDGEMENTS

THE ISLAMIC TEXTS for the Blind (Kitaba) acknowledge the great work of Muhammad Mlamali Adam in initiating the translation of *al-Nasâih al-Dîniyyah* upon which this production is based. It acknowledges the work of its team and all its supporters and helpers in particular the communities in Glasgow, Oslo, Copenhagen and Singapore. Al-Habib Hasan al-Attas, Nasrudin Shafawi, Athar Akram, Farhat Khan, Mehmet Yurdal, Showaib Nabi, Arslaan Khan, Aminah Hussain, Sayka Hussain, Balal Hussain and Adnan Tariq all deserve special mention. It is grateful to the Dollie family, Fatima, Abduraghman, Qasim and Uzair as well as Najma Merchant for proofreading the various stages of the text. By Allah is enabling success.

Kitaba acknowledges the influence of its founding chairman, Imran Sabir and asks Allah to bless his soul and grant this project success.

~❦~

FOREWORD

BY AL-HABIB HASAN BIN MUHAMMAD AL-ATTAS, IMAM OF
BA 'ALAWI MOSQUE, SINGAPORE

I F A PERSON is directed to do something good that will benefit others, he does so only because of his *ikhlâs* (sincerity) and because of *hidâyah* (guidance) from Almighty God. As He says in the Holy Qur'an (2:213): **"God guided those whom he pleases to the straight path."** In another verse (2:269), God says: **"He grants wisdom to whom He pleases; and he to whom wisdom is granted, receives indeed a benefit overflowing."**

When Abdul Aziz Ahmed Fredericks chose to translate the *Nasâih* of Imâm Abdullah bin 'Alawi al-Haddâd, no doubt it was due to his sincere intention that many English-speaking readers would be guided to be closer to Almighty God and to the Holy Prophet Muhammad, upon him be peace. The *Nasâih* is a book designed for the layman, to make him both more knowledgeable and a better person. Using pearls of wisdom from the verses of the Holy Qur'an and the traditions of the Prophet Muhammad, upon him be peace, and with simple and lucid explanations, Imâm al-Haddâd leads the reader away from the world of darkness towards a world of brightness, tranquility and happiness.

Imâm al-Haddâd begins the *Nasâih* with a discourse on *taqwa* (piety) – the key to absolute guidance from the Almighty. In *taqwa*, there is *tauhid* (oneness of God), *imân* (faith), *'amâl* (good deeds) and *ikhlâs* (sincerity). These values are from the chest of treasures that lead to happiness in this world and the Hereafter. Imâm al-Haddâd ends the *Nasâih* with the advice to hold steadfastly to the *aqîdah* (creed) of the *Ahl Sunnah wal Jamâ'ah* and to seven specific traditions of the Holy Prophet Muhammad, upon him be peace. These traditions give us learning from the past and guidance for the present towards the future.

In the world of Islamic scholarship, Imâm al-Haddâd needs no introduction. His writings, *awrâd* (litanies) and *qasâ'id* (poetry) have been well read for more than four hundred years. Imâm al-Haddâd carved a special relationship with our beloved Prophet that is recognized all over the Muslim world, especially among the scholars. One of his magnificent poems graces the columns of the gates of his tomb in the heart of Masjid al-Nabawi in Madinah. It reads:

The Prophet, mighty in character whose character is that which
The Most Merciful glorified in the master of all books

Imâm al-Haddâd was born in Tarîm in the month of Safar 1044H and passed away in the month of Dhul Qada 1132H at the advanced age of 88 years. Though blind, Imâm al-Haddâd memorized the Holy Qur'an in his childhood. He received his religious training from many scholars in Hadramaut, South Yemen – scholars who could trace their lineage directly to the Prophet Muhammad, upon him be peace. He was known for his vast knowledge and humility. Once, a man came to him with money, asking to build a mosque. Imâm al-Haddâd asked him, "Rather than name the mosque after you, can I name it after someone else instead?" The man replied, "Definitely not!" Imâm al-Haddâd said, "Then, you should not build a mosque, as you are not sincere in building it." On another occasion, a man, dressed as a learned scholar with a turban and robe entered a gathering. Imâm al-Haddâd asked who he was. He replied that he was 'the son of so and so'. To this, Imâm al-Haddâd said, "That was your father, the pious and the learned, but who are you? You should wear the dress of a scholar only if you are one, not otherwise." Such was the teaching of the great Sufi, and it is wisdom such as this that Abdul Aziz Ahmed Fredericks makes accessible now to a wider audience in his translation of the *Nasâih* of Imâm 'Abdullah bin 'Alawi al-Haddâd.

TRANSLATOR'S
INTRODUCTION

THE MEANING OF THE WORD *TAQWA*

ALL PRAISE is due to Allah, Lord of the Worlds who gathered all good in *taqwa* and who sent Muhammad, upon him be peace, as the Imâm of the people of *taqwa*. We have deliberately left the word *taqwa* untranslated as we feel there is no exact equivalent in English. Those who have translated it have used a variety of words including 'fear of God', 'awareness of God', 'piety', 'righteousness', 'obedience' and 'devotion'. Each of these translations touches on part of the meaning but does not encompass it fully. Rather than use an inadequate translation, we feel that a brief explanation in the introduction might allow us to use the transliterated Arabic word in the body of the text. The author clarifies the meaning early in the book and hopefully by the end of it, the Quranic concept will be clear to its readers.

Arabic words are formed from three root letters. By tracing a word to its root and examining how the form is extracted, the true meaning can be found. The origin of the word *taqwa* is from the Arabic letters '*qaf*', '*waw*' and '*ya*' and its root means 'to guard against', 'to shield' and 'to place a barrier between oneself and danger'. The word *waqâya*, shield and *wâqin*, 'guardian or protector' or 'means of protection' such as a rain coat (*mi'taf wâqin*) or gas mask (*qanâ wâqin*) are all derived from the same origin.

Imâm al-Haddâd explains that *taqwa* is 'fulfilling the commandments of Allah and avoiding His prohibitions both inwardly and outwardly while feeling adoration and reverence for Allah as well as awe, fear and dread.' Fulfilling His commands puts a 'shield' between oneself and His wrath and the Fire. It is a 'means of protection' and, according to the Imâm's definition, could perhaps be translated as the 'devotion', 'righteousness' or 'piety' that 'protects one from the displeasure of the Lord and any retribution'. This devotion is the consequence of 'reverence' and 'awe'. In this sense it might be translated as the 'awareness of God', 'fear of God' or 'awe' that leads to devotion.

As the translator is not qualified to translate Quranic verses into English, he has adopted the translation of Abdullah Yusuf Ali and has maintained whatever word Yusuf Ali has used in his original work for the word *taqwa*. This has usually been 'fear'. Occasionally phrases such as 'believeth' have been changed to 'believes' to aid the flow of the text.

IMÂM AL-HADDÂD

'Abdullah bin 'Alawi al-Haddâd was a descendent of the Prophet Muhammad, upon him be peace, whose forefathers settled in the Hadramaut valley of Southern Arabia. Those forefathers established a strong tradition of knowledge and calling people to God through their words, actions and writings. They stood for the orthodox Islam of the people of the Quran and Sunnah with a strong emphasis on spiritual growth and good character. Their teachings were influenced by scholars such as al-Ghazâli and Abu Tâlib al-Makki.[1]

Imâm al-Haddâd was born to two of the most upright and saintly people of the time. His parents, 'Alawi bin Muhammad al-Haddâd and Salma bint 'Umar al-Munaffar, were known for their spirituality as well as their knowledge of the legal system and tradition of Islam. The noble Salma gave birth to our Imâm 'Abdullah on 5th Safar 1044H, 1st August 1634 CE. Aged three, Imâm al-Haddâd became ill and lost his sight. Although there were fears that becoming blind might hamper his spiritual and intellectual growth it seemed to have had the opposite effect. His teachers noted an increase in his eagerness and ability to memorise the Quran and other texts and an increase in his devotional worship. His childhood friend, Abdullah Bal-Faqih used to say, 'although our performance of worship was together, Abdullah would always surpass us.' Even as a young child he used to perform between a hundred and two hundred additional prayer cycles every morning. By the age of fifteen, he had studied under almost all the scholars of the area and was eagerly memorising major texts, including the Shafi' law manual *al-Irshâd*. It is reported that he studied under 140 different scholars. After mastering the outer Islamic sciences, his interest was initially not on teaching but on

1   Abu Tâlib al-Makki was an ascetic scholar born in Iraq where he died in 386H/ 996 CE. His most famous book, *Qût al-Qulûb, Provision of the Hearts*, describes the spiritual dimension of worship. Imâm Abu Hâmid al-Ghazâli gathered knowledge of the outer and inner sciences of Islam in his various books but most importantly in a collection entitled *Ihyâ 'Ulûm al-Dîn, Revival of the Islamic Sciences*. He died near Tabiran in modern day Iran in 505H/ 1111CE.

retreat from the world. At seventeen years old, he took to long periods of seclusion in the mosque of al-Hâjira in Tarîm. For a while he refused pleas to teach, but eventually succumbed to the request of a sincere student from the Ba Fadl clan and a relative named Hasan al-Jifrî. Once he began teaching, his thirst for knowledge increased once again and he dedicated himself to teaching, studying and calling people to God.

He was kind and loving and cared a great deal for his community. He was particularly concerned about the poor, widows and orphans. On the rare occasions where he became annoyed with his own servant, he would give him a present to abate his own anger prompting his servant to remark, 'I wish he would be annoyed with me more often.'

In 1079H, 1668 CE, the Imâm performed the pilgrimage to Makkah and visited his noble grandfather, upon him be peace, in Madina. He met many of the world's leading scholars and returned invigorated by the intellectual and spiritual experience. After his return, he settled in al-Hâwi on the outskirts of Tarîm where he established a mosque and his new home. This became the centre of his teaching activities and calling to God. He wrote many books and guided people through direct spiritual training, teaching and litanies which are read today all over the world. He would go out to visit remote villages, teach people at home and write to the rulers and governors. It was because of his tremendous effort in calling to God that he earned the title '*Qutb al-da'wah wal-Irshâd*', the Pole of Calling and Guidance.

He continued teaching and calling to God until his death on 7th Dhul Qada 1132, 12 August 1720 CE. May Allah be pleased with him and benefit us by him.

AL-NASÂIH AL-DÎNIYYAH

RELIGIOUS ADVICE

Imâm al-Haddâd wrote the book *al-Nasâih al-Dîniyyah* in the year he performed the pilgrimage, 1079H. In fact, the section translated in this book and the next portion on worship was written before he left Hadramaut and was read to his noble grandfather, upon him be peace, in Madina. The remainder of the book was composed on the journey or after his return. One of the scholars of the Sacred Cities remarked 'this is the essence of the *Ihyâ*,' meaning that it encompassed the Islamic masterpiece known as *Ihyâ 'Ulûm al-Dîn, The Revival of the Religious Sciences*, by Imâm al-Ghazâli. The Mufti of Syria was on the pilgrimage that year. When he returned to his homeland, he remarked about Imâm al-Haddâd that there was 'no one on the face of the earth like him'. He said that he had written a book called *al-Nasâih al-Dîniyyah* which everyone should read.

This is not the first translation into English. My teacher, Shaykh Muhammad Mlamali Adam published the first part of *al-Nasâih al-Dîniyyah* in a private publication entitled *al-'Alawiyya*. Unfortunately, this is no longer available and copies are very difficult to find. The influence of that first publication on this current project cannot be understated. Any good that can be found in anything that I have translated should be attributed to Shaykh Muhammad Adam and of course the many faults and weaknesses are purely my own. For these, I ask Allah's forgiveness.

The first Malaysian translation divided the book into sections and for this reason we feel justified in publishing the book in parts. It also makes it easier for us to make the message of the Imâm accessible. We are very keen that Imâm al-Haddâd's tradition of providing knowledge and spiritual guidance to all, regardless of their physical state and means, should continue. We at The Islamic Texts for the Blind make our publications available in audio and Braille formats and this is easier with shorter publications. We also believe it makes the book more accessible to our modern readers whose time and dedication to sacred knowledge is not as it had been in previous generations. And by Allah is enabling success.

ISLAMIC TEXTS FOR THE BLIND AND ACCESSIBLE TEXTS

The Islamic Texts for the Blind is a social enterprise project which aims to make traditional Islamic texts accessible to the Blind. It is registered as a charity in Scotland and generates funds from its publications and donations to provide Braille and audio material as well as online classes, lectures and conferences serving the Blind and promoting social inclusion. Its website, www.kitaba.org is fully accessible to those who use screen readers and contains Islamic resources, news and information on Blindness and the Muslim community. We appreciate your support and ask for your prayers for the success of our project and work.

AUTHOR'S INTRODUCTION
TO HIS BOOK
AL-NASÂIH AL-DÎNIYYAH

ND THERE is no strength and no power except by Allah, Most High, Most Mighty. Transcendent are You! We possess no knowledge except that which You have taught us for surely You are the All-Knowing and All-Wise.

All praise is due to Allah, Lord of the Worlds, who made the call to guidance, the indicating of good and sincere advice to the Muslims among the best acts of proximity and highest ranks and most important concerns of the religion. This is the way of the prophets, messengers, righteous saints and the scholars who act upon what they know and are firm in their knowledge and certainty. Allah sends salutations and prayers upon our master and liege lord Muhammad, the Truthful Messenger, the steadfast Beloved One, Seal of the Prophets, Leader of the Righteous, the Master of the Early and Later Ones and likewise upon his family and truthful and sincere companions and also upon those who follow them until the Day of Recompense.

After the aforementioned, the Messenger of Allah, upon him be peace, has indeed said: 'Actions are but by intention and every person will have what he intended and so whoever's migration was for the sake of Allah and His Messenger, his migration was indeed for Allah and His Messenger and whoever's migration was for gain of some worldly benefit or to marry a woman, his migration will be for what he migrated.'[2] And he upon whom be prayers and salutations said: 'Religion is sincerity.' They said, 'to whom, O Messenger of Allah?' He said, 'to Allah, His Book, His Messenger, the leaders of the Muslims and their common folk.'[3]

This is a book that we have authored; in it we have gathered a selection of religious advice and faithful counsel. In this we have intended to benefit ourselves

---

2 Related by al-Bukhâri in the *Book of How the Revelation Began* (*hadîth* number 1) and Muslim in the *Book of Zakât* (*hadîth* number 1907).

3 Related by Muslim in the *Book of Faith* (*hadîth* number 55).

and others and to remind ourselves and our Muslim brethren. We have done so in a simple and uncomplicated manner using easy to understand language so that it can be understood by the elite and the general populace of the people of Islam and faith. We have called the book *al-Nasâih al-Dîniyyah wa'l wasâyâ al-imâniyyah, Religious Advice and Faithful Counsel.* We ask Allah, the Exalted, to make it sincerely for His Noble Countenance drawing us close to His Proximity in the Gardens of Bliss and that He magnifies the benefit for us and all our believing brethren for He is indeed capable of that and able do it. Allah is sufficient for us and the most blessed One to entrust. I have no enabling success other than from Allah. Upon Him do I depend and to Him I turn in repentance.

DISCOURSE ON TAQWA

ALLAH, the Exalted says:

وَمَنْ أَصْدَقُ مِنَ اللَّه حَدِيثًا

And whose word can be truer than Allah's?
(al-Nisâ 4:87)

وَمَنْ أَصْدَقُ مِنَ اللَّه قِيلاً

And whose statement can be truer than Allah's?
(al-Nisâ 4:122)

يَا أَيُّهَا الَّذِينَ آمَنُوا اتَّقُوا اللَّهَ حَقَّ تُقَاتِهِ وَلاَ تَمُوتُنَّ إِلاَّ وَأَنْتُم مُّسْلِمُونَ وَاعْتَصِمُوا بِحَبْلِ اللَّهِ جَمِيعًا وَلاَ تَفَرَّقُوا وَاذْكُرُوا نِعْمَةَ اللَّه عَلَيْكُمْ إِذْ كُنتُمْ أَعْدَاءً فَأَلَّفَ بَيْنَ قُلُوبِكُمْ فَأَصْبَحْتُم بِنِعْمَتِهِ إِخْوَانًا وَكُنتُمْ عَلَى شَفَا حُفْرَةٍ مِّنَ النَّارِ فَأَنقَذَكُم مِّنْهَا كَذَلِكَ يُبَيِّنُ اللَّهُ لَكُمْ آيَاتِهِ لَعَلَّكُمْ تَهْتَدُونَ

وَلْتَكُن مِّنكُمْ أُمَّةٌ يَدْعُونَ إِلَى الْخَيْرِ وَيَأْمُرُونَ بِالْمَعْرُوفِ وَيَنْهَوْنَ عَنِ الْمُنكَرِ وَأُوْلَـئِكَ هُمُ الْمُفْلِحُونَ وَلاَ تَكُونُوا كَالَّذِينَ تَفَرَّقُوا وَاخْتَلَفُوا مِن بَعْدِ مَا جَاءَهُمُ الْبَيِّنَاتُ وَأُوْلَـئِكَ لَهُمْ عَذَابٌ عَظِيمٌ

O you who believe! Fear Allah as He should be feared, and die not
except in a state of Islam. And hold fast all together by the rope which
Allah (stretches out for you), and be not divided among yourselves; and
remember with gratitude Allah's favour on you, for you were enemies
and He joined your hearts in love, so that by His Grace you became
brethren, and you were on the brink of the Pit of Fire and He saved you
from it. Thus doth Allah make His signs clear to you: that you may be
guided. And let there arise out of you a band of people inviting to all
that is good, enjoining what is right, and forbidding what is wrong, they
are the ones to attain felicity. Be not like those who are divided amongst
themselves and fall unto disputations after receiving clear signs, for
them is a dreadful penalty.

(Âli-'Imrân 3:104-105)

The words of Allah, the Exalted: '**O you who believe, fear Allah as He
should be feared**' are a command from Him, the Exalted and Majestic, to
His believing servants that they should have *taqwa*, meaning they should be
in obedient loving awe of Him. Allah, the Exalted, has gathered in *taqwa* all
the good things of this temporal world and the everlasting one. Allah has
commanded His believing servants in this way so that they may succeed and
attain felicity and prosperity through it. He has done this as a mercy to His
believing servants and '**And He is full of Mercy to believers**'.[1]

Taqwa, is the counsel of Allah, Lord of the Worlds to the first people and
the last. Allah, the Exalted said:

$$\text{وَلَقَدْ وَصَّيْنَا الَّذِينَ أُوتُوا الْكِتَابَ مِن قَبْلِكُمْ وَإِيَّاكُمْ أَنِ اتَّقُوا اللَّهَ}$$

**Verily, We have directed the people of the Book before you,
and you (O Muslims) to fear Allah.**

(al-Nisâ 131)

There is no good, neither worldly nor eternal, neither clear nor hidden,
except that *taqwa* provides the access and means to it. Equally, there is no evil,
now or later, open or hidden except *taqwa* provides an impregnable fortress
that grants protection from it and ensures deliverance from its harm.

How many enormous blessings and immense felicities has Allah the Mighty
connected to *taqwa* in His Almighty Book? Among them are 'being with' Allah
in a divine, subtle 'withness' described when He, the Exalted said:

$$\text{وَاتَّقُوا اللَّهَ وَاعْلَمُوا أَنَّ اللَّهَ مَعَ الْمُتَّقِينَ}$$

1   Al-Ahzâb 23:43.

4

But fear Allah,
and know that Allah is with those who restrain themselves.
(al-Baqara 2: 194)

Among them is divine knowledge (*al-'Ilm al-laduni*). Allah, the Exalted
has said:

$$\text{وَاتَّقُواْ اللَّهَ وَيُعَلِّمُكُمُ اللَّهُ وَاللَّهُ بِكُلِّ شَيْءٍ عَلِيمٌ}$$

So fear Allah. For it is Allah that teaches you,
and Allah is well-acquainted with all things'
(al-Baqara 2:282)

And among them is discernment at times of confusion and ambiguity and
expiation of one's transgressions and forgiveness of sins. Allah, the Exalted
has said:

$$\text{يَا أَيُّهَا الَّذِينَ آمَنُواْ إِن تَتَّقُواْ اللَّهَ يَجْعَل لَّكُمْ فُرْقَاناً}$$

$$\text{وَيُكَفِّرْ عَنكُمْ سَيِّئَاتِكُمْ وَيَغْفِرْ لَكُمْ وَاللَّهُ ذُو الْفَضْلِ الْعَظِيمِ}$$

O you who believe, if you fear Allah, He will grant you a Criterion,
remove from you all evil and forgive you.
For Allah is the Lord of Grace unbounded.
(a l-Anfâl 8:29)

Among them is salvation from the Fire. Allah, the Exalted said:

$$\text{وَإِن مِّنكُمْ إِلَّا وَارِدُهَا كَانَ عَلَى رَبِّكَ حَتْماً مَّقْضِيّاً}$$

$$\text{ثُمَّ نُنَجِّي الَّذِينَ اتَّقَوا وَّنَذَرُ الظَّالِمِينَ فِيهَا جِثِيّاً}$$

Not one of you but will pass over it: this is, with your Lord, a Decree
which must be accomplished. But We shall save those who guard against
evil and We shall leave wrong-doers therein, (humbled) to their knees.
(Maryam 19:71-72)

And He said:

$$\text{وَيُنَجِّي اللَّهُ الَّذِينَ اتَّقَوا بِمَفَازَتِهِمْ لَا يَمَسُّهُمُ السُّوءُ وَلَا هُمْ يَحْزَنُونَ}$$

But Allah will deliver the righteous to their place of salvation:
no evil shall touch them, nor shall they grieve.
(al-Zumar 39:61)

And among them is relief from difficulties, provision from unanticipated sources, ease and immense reward. Allah, the Exalted, said:

$$وَمَن يَتَّقِ اللَّهَ يَجْعَل لَّهُ مَخْرَجًا$$

$$وَيَرْزُقْهُ مِنْ حَيْثُ لَا يَحْتَسِبُ$$

And for those who fear Allah, He ever prepares a way out.
And He provides for him from (sources) he never could imagine.
(al-Talâq 65:2-3)

$$وَمَن يَتَّقِ اللَّهَ يَجْعَل لَّهُ مِنْ أَمْرِهِ يُسْرًا$$

And for those who fear Allah, He will make their path easy.
(al-Talâq 65:4)

$$وَمَن يَتَّقِ اللَّهَ يُكَفِّرْ عَنْهُ سَيِّئَاتِهِ وَيُعْظِمْ لَهُ أَجْرًا$$

And if anyone fears Allah, He will remove his ills from him, and will enlarge his reward.
(al-Talâq 65:4)

And among them is the promise of the Garden. Allah the Exalted said:

$$تِلْكَ الْجَنَّةُ الَّتِي نُورِثُ مِنْ عِبَادِنَا مَن كَانَ تَقِيًّا$$

Such is the Garden which We give as an inheritance to those of our servants who guard against evil.
(Maryam 19:63)

And the Exalted said:

$$مَّثَلُ الْجَنَّةِ الَّتِي وُعِدَ الْمُتَّقُونَ$$

There is a parable of the Garden which the righteous are promised.
(al-Ra'd 13:35)

$$وَأُزْلِفَتِ الْجَنَّةُ لِلْمُتَّقِينَ$$

To the righteous, the Garden will be brought near.
(al-Shu'arâ ' 26:90)

$$إِنَّ لِلْمُتَّقِينَ عِندَ رَبِّهِمْ جَنَّاتِ النَّعِيمِ$$

**Verily, for the Righteous are Gardens of Delight,
in the Presence of their Lord.**
(al-Qalam 68:34)

إِنَّ الْمُتَّقِينَ فِي جَنَّاتٍ وَنَهَرٍ

فِي مَقْعَدِ صِدْقٍ عِندَ مَلِيكٍ مُّقْتَدِرٍ

**As to the Righteous, they will be in the midst of Gardens and Rivers in
an Assembly of Truth in the presence of a Sovereign Omnipotent.**
(al-Qamar 54: 54-55)

Among them are nobility and honour (*al-karâma*) in this world and the
next. Allah the Exalted said:

إِنَّ أَكْرَمَكُمْ عِندَ اللَّهِ أَتْقَاكُمْ

**Verily, the most honoured of you in the sight of Allah is (he who is) the
most righteous of you.**
(al-Hujurât 49:130)

He has based honour in His sight on *taqwa*, not on ancestry, wealth or some
other thing. How many blessings, felicities, high ranks, benefits, successes,
bounties and profits has He and His Messenger promised for the (people
of) *taqwa*? It is impossible to count or list them. How beautiful are the word
of the one who said:

مَن يَتَّقِ اللَّهَ فَذَاكَ الَّذِي   سِيقَ إِلَيْهِ الْمَتْجَرُ الرَّابِحُ

Who fears Allah – he is the one
To whom profitable trade comes

It has also been said:

مَنْ عَرَفَ اللَّهَ فَلَمْ تُغْنِه   مَعْرِفَةُ اللَّهِ فَذَاكَ الشَّقِي

مَا ضَرَّ ذَا الطَّاعَةِ مَا نَالَهُ   فِي طَاعَةِ اللَّهِ وماذا لَقِي

مَا يَصْنَعُ الْعَبْدُ بِعِزِّ الْغِنِي   وَالْعِزُّ كُلُّ الْعِزِّ لِلْمُتَّقِي

Who knows Allah yet is not enriched
By awareness of Allah is indeed wretched

7

The man of obedience in his obedience
Will not be harmed, come what may
What will the slave do with the power of riches
When all glory is the glory of the one who has *taqwa?*

SCHOLARS' STATEMENTS ABOUT *TAQWA*

The scholars, may Allah's satisfaction be upon them, say that *taqwa* can be explained as 'fulfilling the commandments of Allah and avoiding His prohibitions both inwardly and outwardly while feeling adoration and reverence for Allah as well as awe, fear and dread.'

Some commentators of the Qur'an, may Allah show them mercy, have said: '**Fear Allah as He should be feared**' means that 'He should be obeyed and not disobeyed, remembered and not forgotten and be rendered gratitude and not denied.'

The servant will never be able to show *taqwa* to Allah as He deserves to be shown even if he were to have a million souls with a million years to each life span and he spent them all in worship and adoration of Allah. This is because of the magnitude of the rights of Allah upon His servants, the Majesty of His Greatness, the Exaltedness of His Prominence and the Loftiness of His Glory.

The one who was the best and most complete in fulfilling the rights of Allah, Muhammad, upon him be peace, said in his supplication acknowledging his inability to fulfil the praise due to Allah: 'I seek refuge in Your pleasure from Your wrath and in Your pardon from Your punishment and I seek refuge in You from You, for I am unable to praise you as You deserve, for You are as You have praised Yourself.'[2]

Some scholars have said that the words of the Exalted: '**Fear Allah as He must be feared**' has been abrogated by the verse which says: '**So fear Allah as much as you can**'.[3] Other scholars have said that the second verse does not abrogate, but clarifies the intention of the first. This is the correct opinion, God willing. For Allah the Exalted, to whom belongs all praise, would not compel a soul to more than it could bear. He could have done that if He so wished for He can do whatever He wills in His Kingdom and Dominion. The Transcendent One has made things easy and light. As the Exalted said: '**Allah does wish to lighten your difficulties. For man was created weak (in flesh).[4] Allah intends every facility for you; He does not want to put you to difficulties**'.[5]

---

2   Related by Muslim in the *Book of Prayer* (*hadîth* number 222).
3   al-Taghâbun 64: 16.
4   Al-Nisâ 4: 27
5   al-Baqara 2:185.

Imâm al-Ghazâli, may Allah show him mercy, said in his book *al-Ihya*:
'When the Exalted revealed: '**To Allah belongs all that is in the heavens and
on earth. Whether you show what is in your minds or conceal it, Allah calls
you into account for it**', the companions of the Prophet, Allah bless them and
grant them peace and may He be pleased with them, considered the verse a
great burden. They approached him and said 'we have been charged beyond
our means'. They understood the verse meant that even the inner whisperings
of the soul would be taken into account. He, upon him be peace, said: 'Do
you wish to say what the Children of Israel said, "we have heard but disobey"?
Say "we hear and we obey, Your Forgiveness, O Lord, and to You is the end of
all journeys.' They said it and then Allah revealed the following verses:

آمَنَ الرَّسُولُ بِمَا أُنزِلَ إِلَيْهِ مِن رَّبِّهِ وَالْمُؤْمِنُونَ كُلٌّ آمَنَ بِاللّهِ وَمَلَائِكَتِهِ وَكُتُبِهِ وَرُسُلِهِ لَا
نُفَرِّقُ بَيْنَ أَحَدٍ مِّن رُّسُلِهِ وَقَالُواْ سَمِعْنَا وَأَطَعْنَا غُفْرَانَكَ رَبَّنَا وَإِلَيْكَ الْمَصِيرُ

**The Messenger believes in what has been revealed to him from his
Lord, as do the men of faith. Each one (of them) believes in Allah, His
angels, His books, and His apostles. "We make no distinction (they say)
between one and another of His apostles." And they say: "We hear, and
we obey: (We seek) Your forgiveness, our Lord, and to You is the end of
all journeys.**
(Al-Baqara 2:286)

He related (their words) and subsequent supplications to show that they
would not be taken to account for forgetfulness and mistakes and that they
would not be burdened beyond their capacity. He answered them, eased their
burdens, lifted their concerns and for that He deserves much thanks.

He, upon whom be peace, further clarified this point saying 'my nation
have been conceded, for my sake, their mistakes, forgetfulness and that which
they were compelled to do.'[6]

༄

The Exalted said: '**Then die not except in the Faith of Islam**'[7]. This is a
command from Him - Transcendent is He – to die upon Islam. This is the
religion of Allah which He informed us is the correct way (*dîn*) with Him.
No other way will be accepted from anyone. It is the religion that He chose
for His Messenger and the believing Servants. The Exalted has said:

6   Related by Ibn Mâjah in *The Book of Divorce* (*hadîth* number 2043).
7   Âli Imrân 3:102.

9

إِنَّ الدِّينَ عِندَ اللّه الإِسْلَامُ

The Religion before Allah is Islam (submission to His Will).
(Âli-'Imrân 3:19)

And He said:

وَمَن يَبْتَغِ غَيْرَ الإِسْلَامِ دِينًا فَلَن يُقْبَلَ مِنْهُ وَهُوَ فِي الآخِرَةِ مِنَ الْخَاسِرِينَ

If anyone desires a religion other than Islam never will it be accepted of him; and in the Hereafter he will be in the ranks of those who have lost (all spiritual good).
(Âli-'Imrân 3:85)

And the Exalted said:

الْيَوْمَ أَكْمَلْتُ لَكُمْ دِينَكُمْ وَأَتْمَمْتُ عَلَيْكُمْ نِعْمَتِي وَرَضِيتُ لَكُمُ الإِسْلَامَ دِينًا

This day have I perfected your religion for you, completed My favour upon you and have chosen for you Islam as your religion.
(Al-Mâida 5:3)

One is not able to bring about one's own death in Islam; however, Allah has prepared a path leading to such an end. If one follows it, then one would have fulfilled his responsibility and the command (to die in Islam). He should prefer death in Islam and should cherish hope for it and be determined to achieve it. He should hate the thought of dying on any other path and always humbly pray and beg that Allah takes his soul in a state of submission. That is how He described His prophets and righteous servants. He informed us about Yûsuf ibn Yaqûb (Joseph), may peace be upon both of them, saying: **'You are my Protector in this world and in the Hereafter, may you take my soul (at death) as submitting to your Will (as a Muslim) and unite me with the righteous'**[8]. Similarly in respect of Pharaoh's magicians after they believed and were threatened dire reprisals. They supplicated: **'Our Lord! Pour upon us patience and constancy and take our souls unto you as Muslims who bow to your will'**[9]. Allah, the Exalted, relates that Ibrâhim (Abraham) enjoined upon his children that they should endeavour to die in Islam. As did Ya'qûb (Jacob), may peace be upon them all. **'And this was the legacy that Ibrâhim left to his sons and so did Jacob: "O my sons! Allah has chosen the Faith for you; then die not except in the Faith of Islam"**[10].

8   Allah talking about the prophet Joseph in Yusuf 12: 101.
9   Al-A'raf 7: 123.
10   Allah talking about the prophets Abraham and Jacob in Al-Baqara 2: 132.

One must strive to do his utmost to preserve and strengthen his Islam by fulfilling such commands as have been made upon him in obedience to Allah, the Exalted. For whosoever neglects the commands of Allah runs the risk of dying outside Islam. His neglect is a sign of his contempt for the duties of religion and a lax attitude towards them. A Muslim should be on his utmost guard against that.

He must also avoid acts of disobedience and degradation. They weaken one's Islam, cause it to wane, shake its very foundation and expose one to the potential loss of faith at the point of death. This has happened to many who persisted in such acts.

The Exalted, said in this respect:

$$ثُمَّ كَانَ عَاقِبَةَ الَّذِينَ أَسَاؤُوا السُّوأَى أَن كَذَّبُوا بِآيَاتِ اللَّهِ وَكَانُوا بِهَا يَسْتَهْزِؤُونَ$$

In the long run, evil in the extreme will be the end of those who do evil; for that they rejected the Signs of Allah, and held them up to ridicule.

(al-Rûm 30:10)

Reflect upon this and abide by Allah's commandments and avoid what He has forbidden. If you slip into one or the other, then repent to Allah, the Exalted. Be on your utmost guard against persisting in it.

Persist in supplication for a good ending. It has reached us that Shaytân, the accursed Satan, says: 'He breaks my back whosoever prays to Allah to grant him a felicitous end. When will this one bask in the glory of his deeds? I fear he has a firm understanding'.

Be plentiful in your thanks and gratitude for the blessing of Islam, for it is the greatest and most magnificent of blessings. If Allah were to bestow the world in its entirety upon a servant and withhold Islam from him, it would be a calamity. However, was He to bestow Islam upon him and withhold the temporal world from him that would not harm him. This is because the first dies and heads for Hellfire and the second dies and proceeds to Paradise.

You must always be in great fear of a bad end, for Allah, the One who turns hearts, guides whom He Wills and leaves to stray whom He Wills. And it is said in a tradition verified as correct: 'By the One whom there is no god save He, one of you might do the deeds of the people of Paradise and would be within only an arm's length of it and Divine Decree intervenes and he embarks on the deeds of the people of Hellfire and thus he enters it. And surely one of you might do the deeds of the people of Hell until he is within an arm's length of it and Divine Decree intervenes and he embarks upon deeds of the people of Paradise and thus he enters it.'[11] The people of *taqwa* and uprightness find this inspires great fear. What about the people of shortcomings and ambiguity! One of the virtuous predecessors used to say: 'By Allah, no one feels assured that he will not be stripped of his religion except he is stripped of it.' The virtuous predecessors used to be terrified of dying without faith despite their good deeds and their lack of sin. They were so terrified that one went as far as saying: 'Should I be offered death in the Faith of Islam at the door of the room or martyrdom at the door of the house, I would choose death in Islam at the door of the room rather than martyrdom at the door of the house because I do not know what might happen to my heart in between the two points.' And another one said to one of his brothers: 'When death comes to me, sit by my head and observe what happens. If you observe that I have died in Faith, take everything I have and sell it and buy sugar and almonds and distribute them among children. If I die in a different state, let the people know, so that he who prays the funeral prayer upon me does so in the full knowledge of what happened'. He had indicated the signs which differentiate between the two states. The narrator says that he died in the Faith of Islam and did as asked by treating children to sweets. Their anecdotes are many and well known.

Know that an evil end often comes to those who are lax about the compulsory prayers and *zakât*, compulsory alms, and those who seek out the faults of the Muslims, cheat in weights and measures, deceive the Muslims or hide the truth from them or confuse them in their religious and worldly affairs, those who deny the saints (*awliyâ Allah*) or who falsely claim the states and stations of the saints and similar such disreputable things.

Among the most likely to die infelicitously are those who innovate in questions of religion and similarly those who harbour doubt in Allah, His Messenger and in the Day of Judgement. A Muslim needs to take great care to avoid these matters. There is no protection from Allah's Decree except for those to whom He grants His Grace.

O Most Merciful Lord! We beseech you by the Light of Your Glorious Face to let us die in the Faith of Islam and may you join us with the virtuous in a state of wellbeing, O Lord of the Worlds.

‌‌

11   Related by Al-Bukhâri in *The Book of Creation* (*hadîth* number 3036) and Muslim in *The Book of Destiny* (*hadîth* number 2651).

Allah, the Exalted said:

$$\text{وَاعْتَصِمُواْ بِحَبْلِ اللّهِ جَمِيعًا وَلاَ تَفَرَّقُواْ}$$

And hold fast all together by the rope which Allah (stretches out for you), and be not divided.
(Âli-'Imrân 3: 103)

This is a command to hold fast to the Religion of Allah, which is adhering to it and being upright upon it in unity. It is a prohibition against disunity as unity is mercy and disunity is a punishment. The Hand of Allah is with the congregation as stated by he upon whom be peace.

At the foundation of this noble religion are unity, mutual cooperation and speaking with one voice. Disunity and not assisting each other in establishing it leads to its weakening and decline. It is clear that unity in religion is at the root of all good and benefit, whereas disunity is at the root of all harm and tribulation.

〜

The Exalted said:

$$\text{وَاذْكُرُواْ نِعْمَةَ اللّهِ عَلَيْكُمْ إِذْ كُنتُمْ أَعْدَاء فَأَلَّفَ بَيْنَ قُلُوبِكُمْ فَأَصْبَحْتُم بِنِعْمَتِهِ إِخْوَانًا}$$
$$\text{وَكُنتُمْ عَلَىَ شَفَا حُفْرَةٍ مِّنَ النَّارِ فَأَنقَذَكُم مِّنْهَا كَذَلِكَ يُبَيِّنُ اللّهُ لَكُمْ آيَاتِهِ لَعَلَّكُمْ تَهْتَدُونَ}$$

And remember with gratitude Allah's favour on you; for you were enemies and He joined your hearts in love, so that by His Grace, you became brethren; and ye were on the brink of the pit of Fire, and He saved you from it. Thus doth Allah make His Signs clear to you: That ye may be guided.
(Âli-'Imrân 3:103).

This verse is a command to express gratitude to the Exalted for the favour of 'joining hearts in love' after the intense hatred that existed between the tribes of al-'Aws and al-Khazraj. This is a command to the 'Ansâr in particular and the 'Arabs in general. They were locked in feuds, dissension and extortion until Allah sent His Apostle to them, revealed His Book, gathered them together, joined their hearts and ended their rancour, hostility and feuds. As a result, they became, by His blessing, brothers in religion, in support of His Messenger and in honour of His rites. This is one of the favours bestowed upon His Messenger, upon him be peace, in his statement:

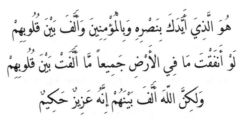

'He it is that has strengthened you with His aid and with (the company of) the Believers. And (morever) He has put affection between their hearts. Not if you had spent all that is in the earth, could you have produced that affection, but Allah has done it: for He is Exalted in might, Wise.'
(al-Anfâl 8: 63)

Indeed, before the Apostle was sent, they were on the edge of the chasm of fire because of their wickedness and idolatry. Allah rescued them by guiding them to His monotheism and obedience. Consequently, Allah, the Transcendent, wanted them to be grateful and acknowledge the rights due to Him as a result of the favour bestowed upon them, that is, the favour of their rescue from waywardness and unity after factionalism.

And He warned them against things that would return them to dissension and discord after harmony and unity: **'Thus doth Allah make His signs clear to you that you may be guided'**, that is so that the guidance you already have leads to further guidance. As Allah, the Exalted says: **'But to those who receive guidance, He increases the (light of) Guidance and bestows upon them their Piety and Restraint (from evil).**[12]

≪≫

The Exalted said: **'Let there arise out of you a band of people'**, meaning a group, **'inviting to all that is good.'**[13] This 'goodness' is a general term that encompasses 'faith and obedience'. Calling to it has a high status with Allah and an act that draw one close to Him. He upon whom be peace said: 'He who calls to guidance gets a reward similar to those who follow him without anything being reduced from theirs; and he who calls to error incurs a sin equal to the sin of his followers, without anything being reduced from theirs.'[14] The Prophet, upon whom be blessings and peace, also said: 'He who points to a good is like he who accomplishes the good.'[15] Whoever makes calling

12   Muhammad 47:17.
13   Âli Imrân 3:104.
14   Related by Muslim in *The Book of Knowledge* (*hadîth* number 2674)
15   Related by al-Tirmidhî (*hadîth* number 2709).

people to good his trait and purpose has taken a great portion from the heritage of the Messenger, upon whom be blessings and peace of Allah, and he treads the path about which Allah, the Exalted, said:

$$\text{قُلْ هَذِهِ سَبِيلِي أَدْعُو إِلَى اللّهِ عَلَى بَصِيرَةٍ أَنَا وَمَنِ اتَّبَعَنِي وَسُبْحَانَ اللّهِ وَمَا أَنَا مِنَ الْمُشْرِكِينَ}$$

Say thou: this is my way: I do invite unto Allah on evidence clear as seeing with one's eyes, I and whoever follows me. Glory to Allah: and never will I join gods with Allah.
(Yusuf 12: 108)

At no time and in no situation was he, upon him be peace, occupied with anything other than calling to Allah. He did so through his words and deeds. It was for this that he was sent. For this he was commanded. As the Exalted said:

$$\text{قُلْ إِنَّمَا أُمِرْتُ أَنْ أَعْبُدَ اللّهَ وَلا أُشْرِكَ بِهِ إِلَيْهِ أَدْعُو وَإِلَيْهِ مَآبِ}$$

Say: "I am commanded to worship Allah, and not to join partners with Him. Unto Him do I call, and unto Him is my return".
(Al-Ra'd 13:36)

The closest and most deserving of people to the Messenger of Allah, upon him be peace, in this world and the next is the one most concerned about this matter and who is most occupied with it and most completely immersed in it. The matter referred to is 'calling to good' which is defined as 'calling to faith and obedience and prohibiting their opposites which are disbelief and disobedience'. Allah the Exalted, continues in His description:

$$\text{وَيَأْمُرُونَ بِالْمَعْرُوفِ وَيَنْهَوْنَ عَنِ الْمُنْكَرِ وَأُوْلَئِكَ هُمُ الْمُفْلِحُونَ}$$

**Enjoining what is right and forbidding what is wrong:
They are the ones to attain felicity.**
(Âli Imrân 3:104)

Felicity means 'the attainment of happiness in this world and the next'.

Enjoining what is right and forbidding what is wrong are among the greatest religious institutions, the most abiding pillars of Islam, and the most important responsibilities of the Muslims. Through them, the affair is established and its good is made complete. Through their neglect, rights are unfulfilled and limits transgressed. Truth becomes hidden and falsehood manifest.

15

'Right' (*ma'rûf*) is a term encompassing everything that Allah has ordered to be done or that He would like His servants to establish. 'Wrong' (*munkar*) is everything that Allah dislikes and would like His servants to avoid. Enjoining right and forbidding wrong is something that has to be established and there is no excuse for not doing so. He, upon whom be peace, said: 'Anyone amongst you who sees a wrong should change it with his hand. If he cannot, then with his tongue. If he cannot, then with his heart, and that indicates a most feeble faith.' And in another version: 'There is not an atom of faith for anything below that', that is, below disapproval with one's heart.

And he, upon whom be peace, said: 'The one who does not respect the elder and does not show mercy to the young and does not enjoin right and forbid evil is not one of us.'

And he, upon whom be blessings and peace: 'By He in Whose Hands is my soul, you will enjoin what is good and forbid what is wrong and you will stop the evildoers or surely Allah will send forth His punishment.'

And he, upon whom be blessings and peace, said: 'When my nation fears to call an evildoer an evildoer, then its good has expired and its damnation has drawn close.'

❧

Allah, the Exalted, does not accept lame excuses and false expediencies which people of our times use to justify their failure to call to what is 'right' and forbid what is 'wrong'. They say, for instance, 'nobody will listen even if we did call to good or forbid wrong' or 'calling to good and forbidding wrong would lead to persecution that we would not be able to bear' and similar things from the imaginings of people who lack insight and have no concern for the way of God.

Silence is permitted when one realistically expects great persecution or when rejection is certain. However, even under such circumstances, enjoining right and forbidding wrong are preferred and appropriate except that they are no longer binding.

The amazing thing is that should one of them be insulted or have some worldly possession taken from him, even if only small, he would not be able to stay silent. He would offer none of the excuses he offers in regards to forbidding wrong. Can this mean anything other than his honour and wealth are more important to him than his religion?

If we accept their statement that no one would listen if they are called to good and forbade wrong, what drives them to consort with and keep company with people who do wrong? Allah has certainly made it compulsory upon them to leave and turn away from them if they do not respond to the call of Allah and His Messenger. It has been established that whoever witnesses wrongdoing and does not work to stop it according to whatever capacity he has is a partner in their wrongdoing. This is the same for one who is content with what they do, even if they are not present with them. In fact, this is the case even if they were the distance of the east from the west. Whoever mixes and consorts with wrongdoers, even if they do not participate in the wrongdoing, will be counted among them by Allah. If punishment befalls them, they will also be affected. They will only be safe if they forbade it and then distanced themselves and parted from them if they refused to accept and continued to reject the truth.

Love for the obedient and aversion for the disobedient for Allah's sake is one of the strongest bonds of faith. It has reached us that the Messenger, upon him be peace, said: 'When the children of Israel innovated religious practices, their scholars forbade them but they did not respond. They continued to mix and eat with them. Once they did that, Allah turned their hearts against one another and cursed them through the tongues of David and Jesus the son of Mary.'

In the story of the village by the sea it is known that they used to fish illegally on the Sabbath. They divided into three groups. One group fished and considered legal that which Allah had forbidden. Another group avoided fishing and forbade them, but did not distance themselves from the wrongdoers. A third group distanced themselves from the wrongdoers and left them after they had admonished them. When punishment was sent to them, it fell upon the first group but also encompassed the second group as they continued to live among the people of disobedience and did not act upon their knowledge. The third group were saved. This is what is referred to in the words of the Exalted:

أَنجَيْنَا الَّذِينَ يَنْهَوْنَ عَنِ السُّوءِ وَأَخَذْنَا الَّذِينَ ظَلَمُواْ بِعَذَابٍ بَئِيسٍ بِمَا كَانُواْ يَفْسُقُونَ

'We rescued those who forbade evil; but We visited the wrong-doers with a grievous punishment because they were given to transgressions'.
(al-A'raf 7: 164)

And Allah turned them into apes and cursed them as mentioned in another verse:

أَوْ نَلْعَنَهُمْ كَمَا لَعَنَّا أَصْحَابَ السَّبْتِ وَكَانَ أَمْرُ اللّهِ مَفْعُولاً

'Or We curse them as We cursed the Sabbath-breakers'.
(al-Nisâ 4: 47).

One flees from and distances oneself from disobedient people once one has lost hope that they will ever accept the call to good.

❧

Know that there is no compulsion upon you to investigate concealed wrong doings. Quite the contrary, it is actually forbidden according to the words of the Exalted: '**And spy not on each other**'[16] and the words of the Prophet, upon him be peace and salutations, 'whoever investigates the secrets of his brother, Allah will investigate his secrets.'[17] All that is obligatory is to enjoin right at the time you see someone neglecting it and the same is true of forbidding wrong. Know this point! For we have seen many who go astray on this issue.

It is important not to believe or accept everything that is related to you about the words and actions of others unless you actually witness it yourself or where that information has come from one who is an upright believer (*mu'min taqiyy*) who does not speculate and only speaks the truth. That is because holding a high opinion of fellow Muslims is an important command. There are many reports made by people against one another. Indulgence has become general. There is little regard for righteousness. Trust has been lost. Gratitude is shown to those who appease their lower desires even if they are not upright upon God's way. Insult is shown to those who contradict even if he is a righteous servant. As a result, praise is given to those who do not deserve it but goes along with the praiser's actions and is silent about wrongdoing. They insult those who contradict them and advise them in the religion. This is the state of the majority. Only those Allah preserves are safe. Therefore, it is necessary to show caution and be circumspect and careful in all affairs. For surely these are trying times and the people have strayed from the truth except those whom Allah wills and they are few.

❧

Know that gentleness, kindness and avoidance of harshness and coarseness are important principles in attracting people to accept and follow the truth. You should show these qualities to those you invite to good and warn away from evil and to those Muslims to whom you offer advice. Be tactful. Speak to them privately and do so with humility because gentleness adorns whatsoever it touches and taints everything which it does not, as he, upon whom be blessings and peace said. Allah, the Exalted, said to His Messenger:

16   Al-Hujarât 49:12.
17   Related by al-Tirmidhi (*hadîth* number 1351).

18

فَبِمَا رَحْمَةٍ مِّنَ اللّه لِنتَ لَهُمْ وَلَوْ كُنتَ فَظًّا غَلِيظَ الْقَلْبِ لاَنفَضُّوا مِنْ حَوْلِكَ

It is part of the Mercy of Allah that you deal gently with them. Were you severe or harsh-hearted, they would have broken away from about you.

(Âli-'Imrân 3: 159)

೩♯०

And the Exalted said:

وَلاَ تَكُونُواْ كَالَّذِينَ تَفَرَّقُواْ وَاخْتَلَفُواْ مِن بَعْدِ مَا جَاءهُمُ الْبَيِّنَاتُ
وَأُوْلَئِكَ لَهُمْ عَذَابٌ عَظِيمٌ

Be not like those who are divided among themselves and fall into disputations after receiving clear signs. For them is a mighty penalty.

(Âli Imrân 3:105)

This is a prohibition from Allah to His believing servants not to be like the People of the Book who had formed groups disputing about their religion. 'Those' are the ones who '**fell into disputations**' in their religion and '**for them is a dreadful penalty.**' Contemplate the 'magnitude' – may Allah show you mercy – of the punishment that He, the Mighty, describes as '**mighty**'. Ponder over it and save yourself from it. That is, by holding fast to the Book and tradition of the Messenger, upon him be peace and avoiding perversity and innovation, differing opinions and divisive passions.

Just as the 'People of the Book' splintered into groups and fell into disputes about their religion, this nation has also splintered and fell into disputes just as the Messenger of Allah, upon whom be peace, said: 'The Jews splintered into seventy-one groups and the Christians splintered into seventy-two groups and my nation will splinter into seventy-three groups. All but one will be in the Fire'.[18] This nation has certainly splintered into this number long ago. The prediction of the Truthful One which was inspired by revelation from Allah, has come true. When he, upon whom be peace, was asked which is the 'saved group'. He said, 'the one that is dedicated to that which I and my companions are dedicated.' And he upon whom be blessings and peace then commanded that in time of disputes, one should hold fast to al-sawâd al-'adham which is the consensus of the majority of the Muslims. Thanks is due to Allah that the people of the Sunnah, prophetic way, have been the sawâd

---

18   Related by Abû Dawûd (*hadîth* number 4584 and 4596) and Ibn Mâjah (*hadîth* number 3992).

19

al-'adham from the first generation until this day. It is true that they are, by Allah's bounty, the 'saved group' because of their holding fast to the Book and the prophetic way, which the righteous predecessors and Companions and Followers followed, may Allah's pleasure be with them.

THE CREED THAT PROVIDES DELIVERANCE AND SAFETY

فَإِنَّا والحَمدُ لله قد رَضِينَا بِالله رَبّاً ، وبالإسلام دِيناً ، وَمُحَمَّدٍ نَبِيّاً وَرَسُولاً ، وبالقُرآن إماماً ، وبالكَعبة قِبلَةً و بِالمُؤمِنِينَ إخْوَاناً . وَتَبَرَّأنا مِنْ كلِّ دِينٍ يُخَالِفُ دِينَ الإسْلام، وآمَنّا بِكلِّ كِتَابٍ أنزَلَهُ الله، وبكلِّ رَسُولٍ أرسَلَهُ الله، وبِمَلائكةِ الله، وبالقَدرِ خَيرِه و شَرِّه، وباليَومِ الآخِرِ، وبكلِّ مَا جَاءَ بِه مُحَمَد رَسُول الله صلى الله عَليه وسَلَم عَنْ الله تَعَالي، علي ذلك نَحْيا وعَليه نَمُوتُ، وَعَليه نُبعَثُ إنْ شَاءَ الله مِنْ الآمِنِينَ الَّذِينَ لا خَوفٌ عَليهِم وَلا هُمْ يَحزَنُون، بِفَضْلِكَ اللَّهُمَ يَا رَبَّ العَالمِينَ.

We are, and all praise is due to Allah, pleased with Allah as our Lord, with Islam as our religion and with Muhammad as our Prophet and Messenger; with the Quran as our leader and with the Ka'ba, the Sacred House of Makkah, as our direction and with the believers as our brothers. We dissociate ourselves from every religion that contradicts the religion of Islam. We believe in all the books sent down by Allah, in every Messenger sent by Allah, in Allah's angels and His predetermination, the good and bad thereof; in the Last Day and in all that Muhammad, the Messenger of Allah, brought from the Exalted. Upon that do we live and die and upon that we hope to be resurrected by the will of Allah in safety and without fear or sadness, by Your bounty O Allah, O Lord of the Worlds.

The Messenger of Allah, upon him be peace, said: 'One who is pleased with Allah as his Lord, with Islam as his religion and with Muhammad as his messenger has "tasted" the reality of faith.'[19] He, upon whom be prayers and salutations, said: 'Whoever says three times every morning and every evening "radiytu billahi rabban wa bil-Islâmi dînan wa bi Muhammadin nabiyan",

19   Related by Muslim in *The Book of Faith* (*hadîth* number 56).

"I am pleased with Allah as my Lord, with Islam as my religion and with Muhammad as my prophet", Allah must be pleased with him.'[20]

༒

And know, O brothers, that the one who is pleased with Allah as his Lord must also be satisfied with His planning and His choices including the bitter parts of His judgment. He should be satisfied with the provision He has apportioned. He should be steadfast in devotion to Him, fulfilling what He has made obligatory and avoiding what He has forbidden. He should be steadfast in tribulation, grateful for His favours, in loving anticipation of meeting Him, satisfied with Him as Guarantor, Trustee and Protector and sincere in worshipping Him, relying on Him inwardly and outwardly. He should run to no one but Him in matters of importance and turn to no one but Him for the fulfilment of his needs.

One who is pleased with Islam as his religion reveres its sanctities and rites. He continually exerts himself in whatever strengthens and increases his firmness and uprightness including gaining knowledge and action. He aspires to increase in it and is fearful of it being taken from him. He is respectful to its people and averse to those who deny and oppose it.

One who is pleased with Muhammad, upon him be peace, as his prophet imitates him, is guided by him, follows his way (shariah), holds fast to his mode of behaviour (sunnah), recognise his immense due, sends plentiful salutations and prayers upon him, loves his family and companions and invokes prayers of Allah's satisfaction and mercy upon them and is gentle to his nation and sincere in dealing with them.

So, O believer, it is appropriate that you demand of yourself that you attain realisation of some of the meanings mentioned when you say the words radiytu billahi rabban wa bil-Islâmi dînan wa bi Muhammadin nabiyan. Demand of yourself that you adopt these qualities and are not satisfied with mere words for they will be of little consequence, although not entirely void of benefit.

Likewise, you should do the same with all litanies, prayers and the like. You should seek within yourself the realisation of the qualities of their meanings. For example, when you say, 'subhânallah – transcendent is Allah', your heart should be filled with recognition of His Transcendence and Might. With the words 'alhamdullilah – all praise is due to Allah', your heart should be filled with praise and thanks. With the words 'rabbighfirli – O Lord forgive me', your heart should be filled with hope that Allah will forgive you and fear that He may not. Do likewise with all the other prayers.

20   Related by Ibn Mâjah and Ahmed on the authority of Abu Salâm, the servant of the Prophet, upon him be peace.

Strive to have presence of mind with Allah, contemplate the meanings of what you say and aspire to attain the qualities that Allah loves you to have and avoid those He dislikes in you.

HEALING THE HEART

And devote your attention to the heart and your inner state. Indeed he, upon whom be peace, said: 'Allah does not look at your faces and your deeds. He only looks to your hearts and your intentions.'[21]

Make your words a reality through your action. Make your actions a reality through your intention and your sincerity. Make your intention and your sincerity a reality through the purification of your inner being and the soundness of your heart, for your heart is your cardinal point around which all else revolves.

It has been narrated in tradition: 'Beware! In the body is a morsel of flesh when it is sound, the whole body follows suit and becomes sound; and when it sickens, the body sickens likewise. Indeed it is your heart!'[22]

It is an obligation to take care of the heart and to exert an effort to its health and to strengthening it. The heart, known in Arabic as the *qalb*, is susceptible to perturbation, turning and change, known in Arabic as *al-taqallab* so much so that he, upon whom peace said: 'It changes much faster than the cooking pot as it boils.' And he, upon whom be peace of Allah, used to frequently supplicate thus: 'O Changer of hearts, hold my heart steadfastly upon your religion.' And used to say: 'Hearts are in the finger-clasp of the All-Merciful One. If he wills, He holds them steadfastly upon righteousness. And if he wills, they go astray from it.' And when he, upon whom be peace wanted to be emphatic in an oath, he would say: 'No, in the the Name of He who changes hearts.'

The Exalted said the prophet Ibrâhim, His Friend (*Khalîl*), said:

$$\text{يَوْمَ لَا يَنْفَعُ مَالٌ وَلَا بَنُونَ}$$

$$\text{إِلَّا مَنْ أَتَى اللَّهَ بِقَلْبٍ سَلِيمٍ}$$

[And let me not be in disgrace] on the Day when (men) will be raised up, the Day when neither wealth nor sons will avail, but only he (will prosper) that brings to Allah a sound heart.
(al-Shu'ara 26:88-89)

21　Related by Muslim in *The Book of Goodness* (*Birr*), *Keeping Good Ties* (*Sila*) and *Etiquette* (*Adab*) (*hadîth* number 2564).
22　Related by al-Bukhâri in *The Book of Faith* (*hadîth* number 52).

Show the utmost concern – may Allah show you mercy – to come to your Lord
with a heart sound and free from associating partners, hypocrisy, innovation,
vile characteristics like arrogance, ostentation, envy and dishonesty towards
the Muslims and vices of that nature. Seek Allah's assistance and be steadfast.
Work hard and exert yourself and say often:

$$رَبَّنَا لَا تُزِغْ قُلُوبَنَا بَعْدَ إِذْ هَدَيْتَنَا$$

$$وَهَبْ لَنَا مِن لَّدُنكَ رَحْمَةً إِنَّكَ أَنتَ الْوَهَّابُ$$

**Our Lord! Let not our hearts deviate now after Thou hast guided us,
but grant us mercy from Your own Presence; for You are the Grantor of
bounties without measure.**
(Âli Imrân 3:8)

This is how those firm in knowledge from among the believing servants
have been described.

HARDNESS OF THE HEART AND HEEDLESSNESS

Beware of hard-heartedness! It is the coarseness and drying-up of the
heart to such an extent that it is unmoved by admonition, nor is it stirred or
softened by the remembrance of death, promises of Heaven and warnings
of Hell and mention of the states of the Hereafter. He, upon whom be peace
said: 'The thing most distant from Allah, is the hardened heart.'[23] And he,
upon whom be peace, said: 'Wretchedness is in four things – a hardened
heart, a dry eye, greed and long hopes'.[24] So be on guard against these four
things. It has been related in a tradition: 'Know that Allah does not accept
the supplication of a heedless heart.'[25]

A heedless heart is not as bad as a hard heart although it is still blameworthy
and extremely harmful. A heedless heart is one that does not wake or take
heed when admonition and sermons are related to it. It does not turn from
its neglect, heedlessness, preoccupation with folly, foolishness, adornments
of the temporal world and pursuit of its desires. The Exalted said to His
Messenger, upon him be peace:

---

23   Related by al-Tirmidhi with the words, 'the most distant of people is the hard heart' (*hadîth* number 2523).
24   Ibn Hajr mentions this is a *marfu'* hadith related on the authority of Anas by al-Bazzâz. Al-Suyûti says it was related by Abu Nu'aym and Ibn 'Adiy and he considered it to be weak.
25   Related by al-Tirmidhi (*hadîth* number 3612).

وَاذْكُر رَّبَّكَ فِي نَفْسِكَ تَضَرُّعاً وَخِيفَةً وَدُونَ الْجَهْرِ مِنَ الْقَوْلِ
بِالْغُدُوِّ وَالآصَالِ وَلاَ تَكُن مِّنَ الْغَافِلِينَ

**And do thou bring your Lord to remembrance in your very soul, with
humility and in reverence, without loudness in words, in the mornings
and evenings, and be not you of those who are unheedful.**
(al-A'râf 7:205)

He forbade him from being among the heedless as He also forbade him
from following and listening to the neglectful. In the words of the Exalted:

وَلَا تُطِعْ مَنْ أَغْفَلْنَا قَلْبَهُ عَن ذِكْرِنَا وَاتَّبَعَ هَوَاهُ وَكَانَ أَمْرُهُ فُرُطًا

**Nor obey any whose heart We have permitted to neglect the
remembrance of Us, one who follows his desires, whose case has gone
beyond all bounds.**
(al-Kahf 18:28)

A sign of heedlessness is when a servant reads the Quran or listens to it
and is unable to contemplate or try to understand its meanings. He does
not pause to take in its commands and prohibitions and its warnings and
descriptions of the clamour of the Day of Judgement. The same occurs with
regard the sayings of the Messenger, upon him be peace, and the words of
the righteous predecessors, upon them be Allah's pleasure.

A sign of heedlessness is that one does not remember death or what follows
it from the affairs of Next World and the states of felicity and wretchedness.
One does not contemplate such matters.

A sign of heedlessness is that one does not frequent the gatherings of
scholars who know Allah and His religion and remind people about His
days, His signs, His promises and His threats. They are the ones who urge
people to obedience and away from disobedience through their deeds and
words. When they cannot be found, the books that they authored can be a
substitute in their absence.

The world will never, God willing, ever be totally void of them, even if the
mischief and immorality of the times become widespread and the falsehood
and its people appear to take the upper hand and both the general population
and the elect turn their backs on Allah and establishing the truth save the
few that Allah has willed. This is according to the words of the Prophet, upon
him be peace and salutations: 'There will always be a group of my nation
who proclaim the truth without caring who stands in hostility towards them
up until the command of Allah comes (that is until the Last Day).'[26] There

26   Related by al-Bukhâri in *The Book of al-Khums* (*hadîth* number 2948) and by Muslim in *The*

are many traditions and narrations indicating that the earth will never be entirely void of a group of people of truth who hold fast to the Book of Allah and the way of the Prophet (*al-sunnah*) save that they will be very few towards the end of time and that they will be veiled so much so that none but the true seeker and sincere aspirant will know them and be guided by them. And Allah the Exalted knows best.

⚬⚬

Know, O brothers – Allah grant you and us assistance – that the best of hearts and most beloved to Allah is one that is pure and free from falsehood, doubt and evil, and is attentive to truth, guidance, goodness and correctness.

It has been stated in tradition: 'There are four kinds of hearts. There is the pure heart that contains a lamp spreading light and that is the heart of the believer. There is a dark, inverted heart and that is the heart of an unbeliever. There is a heart that hangs from its skin and that is the heart of a hypocrite. And there is a foliated heart containing both the faith of Islam and hypocrisy. The faith it contains is like a tender plant that may be nourished by fresh water and the hypocrisy is like a wound fed by pus and blood. Whichever overwhelms the other gets the better of it.'[27]

I say that the last of these hearts appears to describe the hearts of those believers from the commonality who fall short (in their actions) and are mixed up (in their states).

In has also been stated in tradition that 'faith appears as a glow, and then it grows until it illumines the whole heart. Hypocrisy begins as a black dot and it grows until it darkens the whole heart.' We ask Allah for a wholesome state (*'āfiya*) and that we die upon Islam as Muslims.

Faith increases by continually doing good actions and doing them in abundance and with sincerity. As for hypocrisy, it increases through bad actions which includes neglecting the obligations and embarking on the forbidden. As was stated by the Prophet, upon be peace and salutations: 'He who commits a sin, there imprints in his heart a black spot. If he repents, his heart shines. If he does not, it grows and grows until it covers the whole heart in darkness.'[28] This is the rust which the Exalted, Allah, talks about when He says:

Book of Leadership (al-imāra) (hadîth number 1925).
27   Related by Ahmed and al-Taharâni in *al-Saghir* on the authority of Abû Saîd al-Khudri.
28   Related by Ibn Mâjah in *The Book of Abstinence (al-Zuhd)* (*hadîth* number 4244) and by al-Tirmidhi in *The Book of Exegesis* (*hadîth* number 3460).

$$\text{كَلَّا بَلْ رَانَ عَلَى قُلُوبِهِم مَّا كَانُوا يَكْسِبُونَ}$$

By no means, but in their hearts is that stain of the ill which they do.
(al-Mutafifîn 83:14)

There is nothing more evil and more harmful to a man in this world or the next than sin (*dhunûb*). Almost every type of bad or wicked thing that reaches someone is a result of these acts. As the Exalted has said:

$$\text{وَمَا أَصَابَكُم مِّن مُّصِيبَةٍ فَبِمَا كَسَبَتْ أَيْدِيكُمْ وَيَعْفُو عَن كَثِيرٍ}$$

Whatever misfortune happens to you is because of the things your own hands have wrought, and for many (a sin) He grants forgiveness.
(al-Shûrâ 42:30)

A believer should be on his utmost guard against it and the greatest distance from it and should they befall him he should hasten to repentance and turn to Allah. For surely Allah accepts repentance from His servants and pardons transgressions and knows all you do. Whoever does not repent is indeed from the wrongdoers. They wrong themselves and expose themselves to the wrath of Allah by falling into disobedience and then persisting in it by failing to repent as their Lord commanded promising acceptance. He described Himself in this way in His words:

$$\text{غَافِرِ الذَّنبِ وَقَابِلِ التَّوْبِ شَدِيدِ الْعِقَابِ ذِي الطَّوْلِ لَا إِلَهَ إِلَّا هُوَ إِلَيْهِ الْمَصِيرُ}$$

Who forgives sins, accepts repentance, is strict in punishment and has a long reach (in all things). There is no god but He: to Him is the final goal.
(al-Ghâfir 40:3)

Contemplate this verse – may Allah show you mercy! Consider its noble meanings and subtle secrets that inspire fear and hope and yearning and dread among other emotions.

$$\text{وَمَا يَتَذَكَّرُ إِلَّا مَن يُنِيبُ}$$

$$\text{فَادْعُوا اللَّهَ مُخْلِصِينَ لَهُ الدِّينَ وَلَوْ كَرِهَ الْكَافِرُونَ}$$

**But only those receive admonition who turn (to Allah).
Call you, then, upon Allah with sincere devotion to Him.**
(al-Ghâfir 40:13-14)

26

'Ali ibn Abi Tâlib, may Allah ennoble his face, said: 'On this earth are vessels belonging to Allah and they are the hearts. The best of them is the purest, most firm and most gentle.' He then explained that the 'purest' means purest in certainty (*al-yaqin*), the 'most firm' means the most firm in the religion and the 'most gentle' means the most gentle to the believers'.[29]

I say that certainty (*al-yaqin*) is when faith becomes established in the heart of a believer and takes control of it. It is the tranquillity that Ibrâhim (Abraham) asked his Lord for, as He informed us:

$$قَالَ أَوَلَمْ تُؤْمِن قَالَ بَلَى وَلَكِن لِّيَطْمَئِنَّ قَلْبِي$$

He said: "Do you not then believe?"
He said "Yea, but to satisfy my own heart."
(al-Baqara 2:260)

It is clear that this certainty is the ultimate pinnacle of faith as has been mentioned in the tradition, 'certainty is faith in its entirety.'[30] Nothing has descended from above greater than certainty. Certainty is sufficient wealth. And he, upon whom be peace, said: 'Ask for certainty and well being (*'âfiya*) for no one has been given anything better than well being after being granted certainty.'[31]

As for unyieldingness in the religion (*al-salâba*), it is religious strength and firmness and feeling protective of it to such an extent that one would speak the truth even if it were bitter and that one would not fear the reproach of those who criticise. This is how Allah describes His beloved ones:

$$وَيَقُولُ الَّذِينَ آمَنُوا أَهَؤُلَاءِ الَّذِينَ أَقْسَمُوا بِاللَّهِ جَهْدَ أَيْمَانِهِمْ$$
$$إِنَّهُمْ لَمَعَكُمْ حَبِطَتْ أَعْمَالُهُمْ فَأَصْبَحُوا خَاسِرِينَ$$
$$يَا أَيُّهَا الَّذِينَ آمَنُوا مَن يَرْتَدَّ مِنكُمْ عَن دِينِهِ فَسَوْفَ يَأْتِي اللَّهُ بِقَوْمٍ يُحِبُّهُمْ وَيُحِبُّونَهُ أَذِلَّةٍ$$
$$عَلَى الْمُؤْمِنِينَ أَعِزَّةٍ عَلَى الْكَافِرِينَ يُجَاهِدُونَ فِي سَبِيلِ اللَّهِ وَلَا يَخَافُونَ لَوْمَةَ لَائِمٍ ذَلِكَ$$
$$فَضْلُ اللَّهِ يُؤْتِيهِ مَن يَشَاءُ وَاللَّهُ وَاسِعٌ عَلِيمٌ$$

29 Counted as a *hadîth* by some and related by Ahmed and al-Tabarâni as such but disputed by others.
30 A statement attributed by al-Bukhâri to Ibn Masûd in *The Book of Faith*.
31 Related by al-Tirmidhî (*hadîth* number 3629).

'And those who believe will say: "Are these the men who swore their strongest oaths by Allah that they were with you?" All that they do will be in vain, and they will fall into (nothing but) ruin.

O you who believe! If any from among you turn back from his Faith, soon will Allah produce a people whom He will love as they will love Him, lowly with the believers, mighty against the rejecters, fighting in the way of Allah, and never afraid of the reproaches of such as find fault. That is the grace of Allah, which He will bestow on whom He pleases. And Allah encompasses all and He knows all things.'
(al-Mâida 5:53-54)

GENTLENESS TO THE BELIEVERS

As for gentleness to the believers, it is that you show mercy and compassion to them. These are among the most noble characteristics and best traits. They are among the traits by which Allah described His Messenger

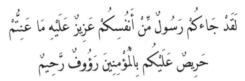

Now hath come unto you a Messenger from amongst yourselves: it grieves him that you should perish: ardently anxious is he over you: to the Believers is he most kind and merciful.
(al-Tauba 9:128)

And the Messenger of Allah, upon him be peace, said: 'The compassionate ones – The Most Compassionate will show compassion to them.'[32] And he also said: 'The spiritual masters (al-abdâl) of my nation do not enter the Garden through their abundant prayers and fasting but by the soundness of their hearts, generosity of their souls and mercy to every Muslim.'[33]

I say: 'One should not understand from this statement that the spiritual masters do not make abundant prayers and fasts. They fast and pray abundantly and do many other righteous acts. Rather, one should understand that the characteristics singled out by the Prophet, upon him be peace, are the ones that propelled them towards the Garden due to their greater virtue

---

32 Related by al-Tirmidhî (hadîth number 1989) and by Abû Dawûd in *The Book of Etiquette* (*Adab*) (hadîth number 4941).
33 Related by al-Bayhaqi in *Branches of Faith* and *al-Mundhiri* in *al-Arbaîn* on the authority of Abu Saîd al-Khudri.

and honour in comparison to other righteous acts. This is because they are actions of the heart and inner qualities and so understand!

The actions of the heart and those of the limbs are never weighed against each other in the scales of good and bad except that the actions of the heart clearly outweigh the actions of the limbs by a considerable amount.

It is as a result of this that the people of spirituality (*ahl al-tassawuf*) who have focused on purification of the heart and its special qualities and on righteous actions have reached ranks that other categories of Muslims have not, including the worshippers and scholars who have not the same concern for the inner affairs. Blessing is in the Hands of Allah and He gives it to whom He wishes and Allah is generous and knowledgeable.

Mercy to the Muslims is a compulsory command and a binding duty. It is even more important in the case of the weak, the poor and those facing tribulations and difficulties. If someone does not find mercy and kindness in his heart when he witnesses the weak among the Muslims and the people of tribulations is hard hearted and overcome by harshness. Mercy has been stripped from him. No one has mercy stripped from him except that he will be among the wretched as mentioned by the one upon whom is peace and salutations.

If, in addition to this harshness, he feels pride in himself, arrogance and a dislike of mixing with the poor and weak Muslims, he becomes remote and distant from Allah and loathed by Him. He deserves to be rejected from Allah's door. He will be reckoned among the arrogant ones who contest with Allah, the Exalted. He, upon whom be peace, said: 'He who has a mustard seed's weight of arrogance in his heart, will not enter the Garden.'

৵৹

Gentleness of the heart incorporates humility and abundant tears out of awe of Allah. This is a noble attribute and praiseworthy conduct. It is the manner in which Allah describes His prophets and righteous servants. The Exalted said:

أُوْلَٰئِكَ الَّذِينَ أَنْعَمَ اللَّهُ عَلَيْهِم مِّنَ النَّبِيِّينَ

مِن ذُرِّيَّةِ آدَمَ وَمِمَّنْ حَمَلْنَا مَعَ نُوحٍ

وَمِن ذُرِّيَّةِ إِبْرَاهِيمَ وَإِسْرَائِيلَ وَمِمَّنْ هَدَيْنَا وَاجْتَبَيْنَا

إِذَا تُتْلَىٰ عَلَيْهِمْ آيَاتُ الرَّحْمَٰنِ خَرُّوا سُجَّدًا وَبُكِيًّا

Those were some of the prophets on whom Allah did bestow His Grace, of the posterity of Adam, and of those who We carried (in the Ark) with Noah, and of the posterity of Abraham and Israel of those whom We guided and chose. Whenever the Signs of (Allah) Most Gracious were rehearsed to them, they would fall down in prostrate adoration and in tears.

(Maryam 19:58)

And the Exalted said:

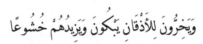

They fall down on their faces in tears, and it increases their (earnest) humility.

(al-Isrâ 17:109)

He, upon him be peace, counted 'a man who remembers Allah while alone and his eyes well with tears' as one of the seven who would be shaded under His Shade on a day when there will be no shade but His.[34] And he, upon whom be peace, said: 'Every eye will cry on the Day of Resurrection except the eye that used to cry out of humility to Allah and an eye that was spent keeping guard while in the way of Allah.'[35] That is while on *jihâd*. Sincere crying out of humility before Allah has been singled out for this rank because of its rarity, despite the abundant crying that people do. The rank is such that he, upon whom be peace, said: 'He who wept out of humility before Allah will not enter the Fire until the milk returns to its udder and the camel passes through the eye of a needle.'[36] And in another narration it mentions 'he who wept tears the size of the head of a fly.' He, upon whom be peace, equated tears wept out of humility before Allah with blood shed in the way of Allah. It has been related: 'If one of the 'nation' (*ummah*) were to cry, He would encompass them all with His mercy as a result of his crying.' This clarifies what we have said regarding the abundance of crying while those who cry purely out of humility before Allah are but few. And so cry out of humility before Allah and if you are unable to naturally cry then strive to cry. Beware of showing off and pretence (of humility) in front of people as through this, you will fall from the grace of Allah, Lord of the Worlds.

❧

34   Related by al-Bukhâri in *The Book of the Community and Leadership* (*al-jama'a wa'l-imâma*) (*hadîth* number 629) and by Muslim in *The Book of the Funeral* (*hadîth* number 923).

35   Related by Abû Nu'aym in *al-Hilya* on the authority of Abû Hurairah and considered by al-Suyûti to be good (*hasan*).

36   Related by al-Tirmidhî (*hadîth* number 1683).

If crying is a rarity for you then contemplate what is before you in terms of the horrors of the next world that you will no doubt encounter. If you indeed believe in Allah and all that Muhammad, the Messenger of Allah, upon him be peace, brought you, you will undoubtedly cry if you possess a heart that understands and an intellect that thinks. And if you do not possess any portion of them, then count yourself among the grazing animals out to pasture and the foraging beasts in the fields. For surely He only addresses and reminds the possessors of hearts. The Exalted has said:

إِنَّ فِي ذَلِكَ لَذِكْرَى لِمَن كَانَ لَهُ قَلْبٌ أَوْ أَلْقَى السَّمْعَ وَهُوَ شَهِيدٌ

**Verily in this is a Message for any that has a heart and understanding
or who gives ear and earnestly witnesses (the truth).**
(Qâf 50:37)

And the Exalted said:

كِتَابٌ أَنزَلْنَاهُ إِلَيْكَ مُبَارَكٌ لِّيَدَّبَّرُوا آيَاتِهِ وَلِيَتَذَكَّرَ أُوْلُوا الْأَلْبَابِ

**(Here is) a Book which We have sent down unto thee, full of blessings,
that they may meditate on its Signs, and that men of understanding may
receive admonition.**
(Sâd 38:29)

And in another place in the Mighty Book:

وَمَا يَذَّكَّرُ إِلَّا أُوْلُوا الْأَلْبَابِ

But none will grasp the Message but men of understanding.
(al-Baqara 2: 269)

And they are the people of intellect. Note the absence of a mention of anyone beside them. In the same way, Allah, the Exalted, has specifically mentioned the people of repentance. They are the ones who turn back to Him, the people of humility who are in awe of Him. They are the people of faith who believe in Him, His Messenger and His threats and promises. And Allah, the Exalted, said:

هُوَ الَّذِي يُرِيكُمْ آيَاتِهِ وَيُنَزِّلُ لَكُم مِّنَ السَّمَاءِ رِزْقًا وَمَا يَتَذَكَّرُ إِلَّا مَن يُنِيبُ

**He it is Who shows you His Signs, and sends down sustenance for you
from the sky: but only those receive admonition who turn (to Allah).**
(al-Ghâfir 40:13)

And the Exalted said:

فَذَكِّرْ إِن نَّفَعَتِ الذِّكْرَى

سَيَذَّكَّرُ مَن يَخْشَى

Therefore give admonition in case the admonition profits (the hearer).
The admonition will be received by those who fear (Allah).
(al-A'la 87: 9-10)

And the Exalted said:

وَذَكِّرْ فَإِنَّ الذِّكْرَى تَنفَعُ الْمُؤْمِنِينَ

But teach (thy Message) for teaching benefits the Believers.
(Al-Dhâriyât 51:55)

He prescribed the act of reminding and commanded the Messenger to it. He made its benefit specific to the believing servants making it an argument in their favour and a path to Him. Likewise, it became an argument against others, demolishing their void contentions. They turned away after they had been given knowledge and denied after they had been made aware. They failed to respond to Allah and His Messenger:

وَقَالُوا قُلُوبُنَا فِي أَكِنَّةٍ مِّمَّا تَدْعُونَا إِلَيْهِ وَفِي آذَانِنَا وَقْرٌ وَمِن بَيْنِنَا وَبَيْنِكَ حِجَابٌ

فَاعْمَلْ إِنَّنَا عَامِلُونَ

They say: "Our hearts are under veils, (concealed) from that to which
thou dost invite us, and in our ears is deafness, and between us and thee
is a screen: so do thou (what thou will) for us, we shall do (what we will!)".
(Fussilat 41:5)

وَأَقْسَمُوا بِاللَّهِ جَهْدَ أَيْمَانِهِمْ لَئِن جَاءَهُمْ نَذِيرٌ لَّيَكُونُنَّ أَهْدَى مِنْ إِحْدَى الْأُمَمِ

فَلَمَّا جَاءَهُمْ نَذِيرٌ مَّا زَادَهُمْ إِلَّا نُفُورًا

They swore their strongest oaths by Allah that if a warner came to them,
they would follow his guidance better than any (other) of the peoples:
But when a warner came to them, it has only increased their flight (from
righteousness).
(Fâtir 35:42)

This description applies to anyone whose Lord has called him to his unity (*tawhîd*) and obedience through the words of His Messenger but who rejected, became arrogant, denied and disbelieved. It also applies to anyone who professed belief with his tongue and outwardly appeared to believe but denied with his heart and was therefore a hypocrite. He will have the same as the disbeliever in terms of Allah's wrath and damnation.

Whoever believes with his heart and professes with his tongue but neglects the duties that Allah has obligated him with and embarks upon the actions of disobedience that Allah has prohibited – his state is one of grave danger. It is feared for him that if Allah does not grant him the enabling success (*al-tawfiq*) to allow him to make sincere repentance before he dies, he will be counted among the hypocrites and disbelievers in Allah's blazing fire, '**that mounts to the hearts. It shall be made into a vault over them in columns outstretched**'.[37]

O obedient believer, be firm in obedience to your Lord. Be abundant in it. Be steadfast. Be sincere in it. And persist in it until you meet Him, the Mighty and Majestic, and He will be pleased with you and you with Him. He will allow you to reside in His abode of nobility.

مَّثَلُ الْجَنَّةِ الَّتِي وُعِدَ الْمُتَّقُونَ تَجْرِي مِن تَحْتِهَا الْأَنْهَارُ أُكُلُهَا دَآئِمٌ وِظِلُّهَا

تِلْكَ عُقْبَى الَّذِينَ اتَّقَوا وَّعُقْبَى الْكَافِرِينَ النَّارُ

The parable of the Garden which the righteous are promised! Beneath it flow rivers: perpetual is the enjoyment thereof and the shade therein: such is the end of the Righteous; and the end of the Unbelievers is the Fire.

(al-Ra'd 13:35)

Pull yourself away – O disobedient believer – from disobeying Him. Turn back to your Lord before death befalls you and you meet your Lord, defiled and tainted. You will be as Allah has said:

قَالَ هُمْ أُولَاء عَلَى أَثَرِي وَعَجِلْتُ إِلَيْكَ رَبِّ لِتَرْضَى

He replied: "Behold, they are close on my footsteps: I hastened to Thee, O my Lord, to please Thee".

(Tâ Hâ 20:84)

You will not be safe from Allah sending punishment upon you unless you hasten to repentance from His disobedience. For the disobedient ones expose themselves to that danger every moment (that they are in disobedience). Do you not hear the words of Allah, the Exalted?

---

37 al-Humaza 104: 7-9.

أَفَأَمِنَ الَّذِينَ مَكَرُوا السَّيِّئَاتِ أَن يَخْسِفَ اللَّهُ بِهِمُ الْأَرْضَ

أَوْ يَأْتِيَهُمُ الْعَذَابُ مِنْ حَيْثُ لَا يَشْعُرُونَ

أَوْ يَأْخُذَهُمْ فِي تَقَلُّبِهِمْ فَمَا هُم بِمُعْجِزِينَ

أَوْ يَأْخُذَهُمْ عَلَى تَخَوُّفٍ فَإِنَّ رَبَّكُمْ لَرَؤُوفٌ رَّحِيمٌ

**Do then those who devise evil (plots) feel secure that Allah will not
cause the earth to swallow them up, or that the Wrath will not seize them
from directions they little perceive? Or that He may not call them to
account in the midst of their goings to and fro, without a chance of their
frustrating Him? Or that He may not call them to account by a process of
slow wastage – for thy Lord is indeed full of kindness and mercy.**
(al-Nahl 16:45-47)

O Allah, make us – O Generous One – from among those who benefit from
Your reminder. Make us from among those who are in compliance with Your
Book and Your Messenger and who gather upon obedience to You. Take our
souls – O Lord – in a state of submission to You and gather us among the
righteous ones. And do likewise with our parents and loved ones through
Your mercy, O Most Merciful of merciful ones.

LENGTHY HOPES

Know, O brothers, may Allah awaken our hearts and your hearts from the
slumber of neglect and enable us and you to prepare for the departure from
the temporal world to the eternal world, that among the most dangerous
things for a person are lengthy hopes.

The meaning of lengthy hopes is 'the feeling that one will last forever in
this temporal world so much so that this feeling takes over the heart and one
acts accordingly.' The righteous predecessors, may Allah show them mercy,
said, 'he who extends his hopes spoils his actions.' This is because lengthy
hopes lead one to covet this temporal world and make one eager to attain it,
so much so that one spends day and night contemplating its acquisition and
development. Considering how to attain it will sometimes be through thought
and sometimes through action. One will strive for it with his exterior and, in
doing so, his heart and body will be immersed in it. At this point, one will
forget the next world and striving for it and procrastinate in actions related to
it. In his worldly matters, he will be eager and enthusiastic and in his religious

duties, he will procrastinate and fall short. It should be the opposite. He should be eager about the next world which is the eternal abode and the place of permanent residence. Allah, the Exalted, informed His Messenger, upon him be peace, that no one attains it except through striving for it, seeking, exertion and zeal for it. As for the temporal world, it is a fleeting place and merely a point of departure. One will soon travel from it to the next world and leave it behind. One is not commanded to seek or covet it. In fact, this is prohibited in the Book of Allah and the way of His Messenger, upon him be peace. The portion of it that has been assigned for him will not miss him even if he does not pursue it. However, when his hopes become lengthy, they lead him to covet this world and procrastinate about the next one. The matter of death does not cross his mind, nor does preparation for it through righteous actions. If it does, he promises himself that he will do them once he is free of some of the worldly preoccupations at some point in the future. He does this as if his lifespan is in his own hands and that he will die when he determines. All of this is a result of the wickedness of lengthy hopes. Take care – may Allah show you mercy – not to show procrastination and delay in your worldly affairs and eagerness and zeal in the affairs of the next world. As the Prophet, upon him be peace, said: 'Work for your worldly affairs as if you will never die and work for the next world as if you will die tomorrow.'[38]

Feel the closeness of death. It is, as mentioned in the tradition, 'the closest of absent things.' One does not know! Perhaps there only remains a short amount of one's lifespan, and he is turning in earnest to this world and turning away from his Hereafter. If death befalls him while he is in this state, he will return to Allah unprepared for meeting Him. Perhaps he will hope for an extension when death comes, but it will not be answered and no exception made. It is as Allah, the Exalted said:

$$ حَتَّى إِذَا جَاءَ أَحَدَهُمُ الْمَوْتُ قَالَ رَبِّ ارْجِعُونِ $$

$$ لَعَلِّي أَعْمَلُ صَالِحًا فِيمَا تَرَكْتُ $$

$$ كَلَّا إِنَّهَا كَلِمَةٌ هُوَ قَائِلُهَا وَمِن وَرَائِهِم بَرْزَخٌ إِلَى يَوْمِ يُبْعَثُونَ $$

(In falsehood will they be) until, when death comes to one of them, he says: "O my Lord! Send me back (to life), in order that I may work righteousness in the things I neglected." "By no means! It is but a word he says." Before them is a Partition till the Day they are raised up.
(al-Mu'minûn 23:99-100)

---

[38] There are a number of traditions, some prophetic, including one related on the authority of Ibn 'Amr by al-Bayhaqi in his *Sunan*.

The one who lengthens his hopes, delays his actions and is neglectful of preparation for death is a deluded fool. The Messenger of Allah, upon him be peace, said: 'The wise one is the one who takes account of himself and works for that which is after death. The incompetent (al-Âjiz) is the one who follows the whims of his lower self and cherishes fond wishes of Allah.'[39] Lengthy hopes are from following the whims of the lower self, delusion and false optimism.

Some of the righteous forefathers, may Allah be pleased with them, said, 'if you were to see the end of one's lifespan and the route to it, you would hate false hope and its deception.' Another said, 'how many welcome a day but do not see its ending? How many hope for tomorrow, but do not reach it?' Another said, 'perhaps one smiles a full smile while his funeral shroud has already left the bleachers.' It has been related in a prophetic tradition: 'The first of this nation will be saved by certainty and renunciation and the last of it will be destroyed by greed and lengthy hopes.'[40]

'Ali, may Allah be pleased with him, said, 'the thing I fear most for you is the following of whims and lengthy hope. As for following whims, it bars you from the truth. Whoever forgets the next world does not work for it. Whoever does not work for it, will come to it and he will be bankrupt of the righteous deeds without which there is no salvation and no success. If he were to then request to be returned to the temporal world so he could perform some good acts, it will be an impossibility. This will magnify his loss and sense of regret at a time when regret will be of no benefit.'

In the advice of the Messenger of Allah, upon him be peace, to Ibn Umar, may Allah be pleased with him, he said: 'Be in the world as if you are a stranger or wayfarer.'[41] This contains the ultimate encouragement to shorten one's hopes and to reduce one's desire for the world. Ibn Umar used to say, 'if you wake in the morning do not anticipate the evening and if you reach the evening do not anticipate the morning. Take from your life for your death and from your health for your sickness.'

CATEGORIES OF PEOPLE WITH REGARD TO LENGTHY HOPES

Know that people fall into three categories with regard to lengthy hopes. The first category consists of the foremost believers (al-Sâbiqûn) which

39   Related by al-Tirmidhî (hadîth number 2586).
40   Related by Ahmed in The Book of Asceticism (Zuhd) and al-Bayhaqi in The Branches of Faith on the authority of Ibn 'Amr.
41   Related by al-Bukhârî in The Book of Subtleties (al-Riqâq) (hadîth number 6053).

includes the prophets and the most righteous ones (*al-Siddîqûn*). They have no worldly anticipation. They are always in a state where they feel their impending death. They are prepared for it by always being oriented towards Allah and His obedience, completely free from preoccupation with the temporal world except for that which is absolutely necessary for themselves or for those they are responsible for. They have reached a level in their orientation to Allah and the next world that if someone were to say to them, 'you are to die tomorrow,' they would not be able to increase the amount of righteous deeds they do. This is because they are at the utmost limit beyond which they cannot increase. Likewise, they would find no thing they need to abstain from because they already abstain from everything one should give up so that death does not catch them in a mixed-up state. What we have mentioned about the first category was alluded to in the words of the one upon whom be peace: 'By Him in Whose hands is my soul, I do not lift my foot except that I do not expect to live long enough to lower it to the ground, nor do I raise a morsel of food except that death might take me before I chew it.'[42] Sometimes he, upon him be peace and salutations, would make the *tayyamum* (sand ablution) even though water was close by. He would say regarding this: 'I do not know! Perhaps I may not reach it.'

The second category consists of the 'middle ranking' among the righteous and virtuous. They have short hopes which do not divert them from Allah and His remembrance. Their hopes do not make them forget the next world nor do they preoccupy them from preparation for death or make them build up the loathsome, temporal world or glorify it or be deluded by its passions and adornments.

However, they have not been given the same strength that the first category have in terms of their feeling that death is about to fall at any moment. If they were in that state of constant anticipation of death, they would not be able to fulfil their necessary ties and perhaps even their religious duties may not be fulfilled due to them being overwhelmed with bewilderment and alarm. For surely, continually feeling imminent death is a mighty state that cannot be carried except through the power of prophethood or the highest state of spirituality known as *al-siddîqiya*.

It is in this respect that it has been said that in hope is a mercy. It refers to this hope without which the worldly and religious affairs would be shaken. This is what has been indicated in the tradition which states that when Allah took out the progeny of Adam on the Day of the Contract, the angels saw their great number and said, 'O Lord, the world will not suffice them all!' And so He, the Exalted, said, 'I have created death.' They then said, 'they

---

42   Related by Ibn Abî Dunyâ in *The Book of Short Hopes* (*Qasr al-amal*), al-Tabarâni in the *Musnad al-Shâmiyîn* and Abû Nu'aym in *al-Hilya*.

will not enjoy life?' And so He said, 'I have created hope.'

It has been related that the Prophet, upon him prayers and salutations (said): 'The angels say to the family of the deceased when they leave his grave, "go about in the world and forget your deceased".' The angels, may peace be upon them, are not supplicating for something bad, meaning lengthy hopes but for something good which are short hopes which provide them with the ability to establish the necessary duties of their life but not to forget the next world. And Allah knows best.

The third category consists of the deluded and foolish ones whose hopes are extremely long, to the extent that they forget the next world. They have diverted them from remembrance of death. They have driven them to orientate themselves with all their hearts towards love of the temporal world, concern for developing it, the gathering of its wares, delusion by its adornment and embellishment and the gazing at its ornamentation which Allah forbade His Prophet from looking at, for the Exalted said:

وَلَا تَمُدَّنَّ عَيْنَيْكَ إِلَى مَا مَتَّعْنَا بِهِ أَزْوَاجًا مِّنْهُمْ زَهْرَةَ الْحَيَاةِ الدُّنْيَا لِنَفْتِنَهُمْ فِيهِ
وَرِزْقُ رَبِّكَ خَيْرٌ وَأَبْقَى

Nor strain your eyes in longing for the things We have given for enjoyment to parties of them, the splendour of the life of this world, through which We test them: but the provision of thy Lord is better and more enduring.

(Tâ Hâ 20:131)

You will see that one in this category hardly remembers death and does not ponder over it. The closeness of death and the nearness of the expiration of one's lifespan does not cross his mind and if it occasionally does, it does not affect his heart. When he fears it will affect his heart, he quickly recalls that which makes him forget it, so that his orientation to the temporal world and his enjoyment of its passions and sensations are not disrupted.

Hope in this form is repulsive and absolutely disapproved of. One who possesses it is of the losers whose possessions and children divert them from the remembrance of Allah and he will be among those who say at their death and when they see the horrors of the afterlife: '**O my Lord why do you not give me respite for a while?**' [43] In this context, Allah has mentioned in His Book saying:

يَا أَيُّهَا الَّذِينَ آمَنُوا لَا تُلْهِكُمْ أَمْوَالُكُمْ وَلَا أَوْلَادُكُمْ عَن ذِكْرِ اللَّهِ

---

43   al-Munâfiqûn 63:10.

وَمَن يَفْعَلْ ذَلِكَ فَأُوْلَئِكَ هُمُ الْخَاسِرُونَ

وَأَنفِقُوا مِن مَّا رَزَقْنَاكُم مِّن قَبْلِ أَن يَأْتِيَ أَحَدَكُمُ الْمَوْتُ فَيَقُولَ رَبِّ لَوْلَا أَخَّرْتَنِي إِلَى

أَجَلٍ قَرِيبٍ فَأَصَّدَّقَ وَأَكُن مِّنَ الصَّالِحِينَ

وَلَن يُؤَخِّرَ اللَّهُ نَفْسًا إِذَا جَاءَ أَجَلُهَا وَاللَّهُ خَبِيرٌ بِمَا تَعْمَلُونَ

'O you who believe! Let not your riches or your children divert you from the remembrance of Allah. If any act thus, the loss is their own. And spend something (in charity) out of the substance which We have bestowed on you, before death should come to any of you and he should say, "O my Lord! Why did You not give me respite for a little while? I should then have given (largely) in charity, and I should have been one of the doers of good".
But to no soul will Allah grant respite when the time appointed (for it) has come; and Allah is well acquainted with (all) that you do.'
(al-Munâfiqûn 63:9-11)

It has reached us that the Angel of Death, upon him be peace, appears to one about to die shortly before his time expires. He says, 'O Angel of Death, give me a little more time so that I can repent to my Lord and seek His forgiveness.' He will say, 'you were already granted a long time and lived long but you did not repent or turn to your Lord until now. The prescribed period is now up and the life span has expired and so delay is not possible.'

Some of the scholars, may Allah show them mercy, have said, 'if he had the whole world in his possession in which to trade an hour or more of his lifespan so that he could make amends to his Lord in it, he would.'

Heedlessness of the next world, total neglect of it and preoccupation with it are the consequences of the lengthy hopes that we have mentioned. They may well also be caused by doubt about the Hereafter and hesitation about its truth – and refuge is sought with Allah from such a thing – and that is indeed part of disbelief in Allah and His Messenger. The sign by which the heedless one may distinguish whether his neglect of the Hereafter is caused by lengthy hopes or doubt, is that when the one whose heedlessness is caused by lengthy hopes becomes ill or is effected by something of that nature which indicates the closeness of death, he remembers death and regrets the time wasted by neglecting good deeds. He hopes that he will recover so that he can do righteous acts. Whereas, one whose neglect is caused by doubt does not experience such feelings or related things while sick. He merely becomes sad about the temporal world leaving him and fears the loss of his children

39

and possessions. This highlights limited perception and a desire for the states of the temporal world. Consider this within yourself – may Allah show you mercy! Examine this in others so that you can advise and warn them if you sense in them the whiff of doubt about the Hereafter. Although doubt in the Hereafter is of a different degree of blameworthiness and danger to lengthy hopes which lead to neglect of the Hereafter, lengthy hopes are extremely blameworthy.

REMEMBRANCE OF DEATH

Know that frequent remembrance of death is recommended and something desirable. It has many majestic benefits including shortening of one's lengthy hopes, renunciation of the temporal world, contentment with very little, desire for the next world and increase in righteous actions. The Messenger of Allah, upon him be peace, said: 'Remember the severer of pleasures frequently.'[44] This refers to death.

He, upon him be peace and salutations, used to rise at night and say: 'Death has come with all that it contains. The convulsion (al-Râjifah) followed by the commotion (al-Râdifah) has come.'[45] When he was asked about the most intelligent of people, he said: 'Those who remember death most often and are best prepared for it. They are the intelligent ones. They have the honour of this world and the blessings of the next.'[46]

I say: The benefit of remembering death is not in just articulating the words, 'death, death'. That would have very little benefit even if done abundantly. Rather what is required is to contemplate with the heart and bring death to mind whenever the words are mentioned. One should think about the states of death and the torments and anguish one will witness in the next world as well as the shortness of one's lifespan, the state one might be in when it expires and one's destination afterwards. Other similar reminders and thoughts are beneficial to the heart and will leave a lasting impression.

Some of our righteous predecessors have said, 'think of the states in which you would like death to come to you and then stick to those actions. Think of all the states you would not like death to come to you and stay away from them.' Ponder – may Allah show you mercy – these words, for they indeed contain enormous benefit for one who acts upon them. And Allah is the one who grants enabling success and assistance. There is no Lord other than Him.

44   Related by al-Tirmidhî (hadîth number 2308).
45   Related by al-Tirmidhî (hadîth number 2574).
46   Related by al-Tabarâni in al-Kabîr and al-Hâkim in al-Mustadrak on the authority of Sa'd ibn Masûd.

As for disliking death, it is natural. A person can hardly go against it. This is because death is, by its nature, painful and it tears a person from his loved ones and the beloved things of his world. The Messenger of Allah said, 'whoever loves to meet Allah, Allah loves to meet him and whoever abhors the meeting with Allah, Allah abhors the meeting with him.' 'Āisha, may Allah be pleased with her, said, 'O Messenger of Allah, we all abhor death?' He, may Allah send him prayers and salutations, said: 'Surely the believer, when death comes to him, is given glad tidings of the Mercy of Allah and so he loves the meeting with Allah and Allah loves the meeting with him. But when death comes to the disbeliever, he is given tidings of a punishment from Allah and therefore he despises the meeting with Allah and Allah despises the meeting with him.'[47] The description of the beloved believer has been mentioned in a divine narration where Allah begins by saying, 'those who draw near do not draw near by the like of what I have made compulsory for him.' The narration reaches a point where Allah the Exalted says: 'I have not hesitated in anything that I do as I do when I take the soul of My believing slave. He dislikes death and I dislike grieving him, but it is inevitable.'[48]

If you look at the aversion to death even though his faith is complete and he has such a high station with the Exalted you will understand the truth of what we have said. In the story of Mûsâ (Moses), it related that he slapped the Angel of Death when he came to take his soul and knocked out his eye.

Indeed! The aversion to death may conceal itself to the point that one does not feel it due to the state of having the lights of gnosis and certainty rise up within. This happens to people from time to time. The general rule with most people of faith is that they love death in that it leads to a meeting with Allah, journeying to the eternal world and departure from the temporal world with all its tribulations and trials. They dislike death which is natural due to its pain and being torn from their loved ones. When the faith is strong, the aversion and natural inclination is less. The inverse is also true. Understand this well and Allah will take guardianship over your guidance.

LONG LIFE

A long life in obedience to Allah is beloved and desirable according to the statement of the one upon whom be peace and salutations: 'The best of you is the one whose life is long and whose actions are good.'[49] The longer

47   Related by al-Bukhâri in *The Book of Subtleties (al-Riqâq)* (*hadîth* number 6142) and Muslim in *The Book of Remembrance, Supplication, Repentance and Asking Forgiveness* (*hadîth* number 2684).
48   Related by al-Bukhâri in *The Book of Subtleties (al-Riqâq)* (*hadîth* number 6137).
49   Related by al-Tirmidhî (*hadîth* number 2431).

the life in obedience to Allah, the more the good deeds and the higher the spiritual level. As for a long life not spent in obedience to Allah, it is a tribulation and is evil, as the bad deeds are increased and the transgressions are multiplied.

If a person claims that he would like to remain in this temporal world for long so that he can increase the number of good deeds that bring him close to Allah, and, at the same time, he is earnest in doing them and concerned about them while avoiding worldly preoccupations, then he is one of the truthful ones. However, if he is lazy and procrastinates in doing them, then he is one of the liars who offer lame excuses. This is because he will have the utmost concern about the thing that is the reason he wishes to remain for, as he will be afraid of losing it or fears something will come between him and it. This is especially true of righteous deeds as they cannot be performed anywhere but in this world. It is inconceivable anywhere else. This is because the next world is the world of recompense not the world of action. Think carefully about this and perhaps it will be of benefit to you. Seek assistance of Allah and be steadfast. Work hard and strive. Rush to righteous acts before you are left with no means to do so. Take advantage of the margin of opportunity before the appointed time comes to you. You are the target of many tests and a target for the slings of death. The only capital you possess to buy eternal felicity is your lifespan. So beware not to spend your time, days, hours and exhalations of breath in things which will be of no benefit for you. If you do, it will lengthen your loss and increase your regret after your death. Then you will know the reality of what you have wasted.

It has been related that in the Hereafter, a person will be shown the hours of his days and nights in the form of vaults. There will be twenty-four vaults corresponding to the hours of his day. He will see the hour that he spent in obedience full of light and the hour that he spent in disobedience filled with darkness. The hour that he did neither obedience nor disobedience will be empty. His sadness will increase when he looks at the hours which are empty and he wishes they were filled with light. When he sees the vaults filled with darkness his grief and distress would be so great that he could die but there is no death in the next world. One who worked in obedience of Allah will be eternally joyously happy. His joy and happiness will increase as time goes by. One who was disobedient to Allah will be in distress and grief. His distress and grief will increase without ending. Therefore, choose what will benefit – may Allah show you mercy – while you are in the abode of choice. For surely, once you have died you will be beyond the matter of choice.

⁓

Make haste and do not procrastinate. Surely procrastination is evil. A person is exposed to trials and many distractions. He, upon him be peace, said: 'Make the most of five before five, your youth before your old age, your health before your sickness, your free time before you become busy, your wealth before your poverty and your life before your death.'[50] And he, may prayers and salutations be upon him, said: 'Hasten to good actions before distractions get the better of you, maintain the relationship between you and your Lord through abundant remembrance of Him.'[51]

And he, may prayers and salutations be upon him, said: 'There are two blessings in which many people are duped. They are health and free time.'[52]

I say: The ones who are duped by these two blessings are those who are given health and free time but spend their health and free time in folly and wastefulness or worldly distractions that divert them away from remembrance of Allah and from righteous deeds. It only becomes clear to them after they die and they see the high levels that they could have attained had they used the health and free time to acquire them.

'Ali, may Allah ennoble his face, said: 'People are asleep. When they die, they wake up.' And Allah, the Exalted said:

$$يَوْمَ يَجْمَعُكُمْ لِيَوْمِ الْجَمْعِ ذَلِكَ يَوْمُ التَّغَابُنِ$$

The Day that He assembles you (all) for a Day of Assembly – that will be a day of mutual loss and gain (among you).
(al-Taghâbun 64:9)

And the Prophet, upon him be peace and salutations, said: 'The people of the Garden will have no regrets except for the hour that passed them and they were not in remembrance of Allah.'[53] That will be when they see the value of what was lost in terms of blessing and proximity as a result of negligence during that hour.

One who spent his health and free time in disobedience of Allah and actions that would anger Him is a loathsome loser rather than just one who was duped. One who is duped is one who only spent his time in folly and things that were permissible. It is possible that the concept of *ghibin* (in loss or duped) in health and free time refers to one who is not given either and the person has been afflicted by illness, weakness or endless preoccupations

50   Related by al-Hâkim in *al-Mustadrak* and al-Bayhaqi in *The Branches of Faith* on the authority of Ibn Abbâs.
51   Related by Ibn Mâjah (*hadîth* number 1081).
52   Related by al-Tirmidhî (*hadîth* number 2405).
53   Related by al-Bukhâri in *The Book of Subtleties* (*al-Riqâq*) (*hadîth* number 6049).

and as a result is unable to do the righteous acts of those who are given health and free time. You should understand the following statement of the Exalted in this context:

$$وَفَضَّلَ اللّٰهُ الْمُجَاهِدِينَ عَلَى الْقَاعِدِينَ أَجْرًا عَظِيمًا$$

But those who strive and fight hath He distinguished above those who sit (at home) by a special reward.
(al-Nisâ 4:95)

And also the words of the one upon whom be peace and salutations: 'A believer who is physically strong is better and more beloved than the one who is physically weak and in both is goodness. Be earnest about the things that benefit you, and seek assistance of Allah and do not be lazy. And if you are overwhelmed by a situation say "Allah plans and acts as He wills". Beware of the phrase "if only" for "if only" opens the doors for the devil.'[54]

I said: This is because the phrase 'if only' is mainly used by someone who is lazy or incapable who has lost the opportunity for something good due to his laziness and inability. He relies on his own ability, capacity, resources and ingenuity. He imagines that he can avoid what Allah has destined through his care and precaution. Indeed, he, upon him be peace and salutations, said: 'Precaution will not avail of what has been pre-determined.'[55] Ponder over this and look to the meanings within it for they are majestic. Beneath them are depths of knowledge. To Allah is the end of all affairs.

WISHING FOR FORGIVENESS

As for hope of forgiveness and the entrance to the Garden without working for it through fulfilling the commands, racing to good deeds, avoidance of the forbidden and distancing oneself from sin, it is foolishness and delusion. It is from befriending the devil who has been cursed by Allah, by accepting his deceit and confusion and his promotion of evil in the guise of good. And the Exalted said:

$$وَمَن يَتَّخِذِ الشَّيْطَانَ وَلِيًّا مِّن دُونِ اللّٰهِ فَقَدْ خَسِرَ خُسْرَانًا مُّبِينًا$$

Whoever, forsaking Allah, takes Satan for a friend, has of a surety, suffered a loss that is manifest.
(al-Nisâ 4:119-120)

54 Related by Muslim in *The Book of Destiny* (*hadîth* number 2664).
55 Related by al-Hâkim in *al-Mustadrak* on the authority of 'Âisha.

One who thinks that he can sin and not repent sincerely to Allah yet expects Him to forgive him while at the same time he is lazy about acts of obedience, preoccupied with affairs of the temporal world imagining that Allah, the Exalted will honour him and raise his rank in the Garden to those of the righteous, is a deluded dreamer and an incapable fool. This is because the Exalted has said and His Word is true:

وَلِلَّهِ مَا فِي السَّمَاوَاتِ وَمَا فِي الْأَرْضِ

لِيَجْزِيَ الَّذِينَ أَسَاؤُوا بِمَا عَمِلُوا وَيَجْزِيَ الَّذِينَ أَحْسَنُوا بِالْحُسْنَى

Yea, to Allah belongs all that is in the heavens and on earth: so that He rewards those who do evil according to their deeds and He rewards those who do goo, with what is best.

(al-Najm 53:31)

Allah described those who do good, in the words of the Exalted:

الَّذِينَ يَجْتَنِبُونَ كَبَائِرَ الْإِثْمِ وَالْفَوَاحِشَ إِلَّا اللَّمَمَ إِنَّ رَبَّكَ وَاسِعُ الْمَغْفِرَةِ

Those who avoid great sins and shameful deeds, only (falling into) small faults, verily thy Lord is ample in forgiveness.

(al-Najm 53:32)

'Small faults' are the minor transgressions that the servant can hardly free himself from. And the Exalted said:

أَمْ نَجْعَلُ الَّذِينَ آمَنُوا وَعَمِلُوا الصَّالِحَاتِ كَالْمُفْسِدِينَ فِي الْأَرْضِ أَمْ نَجْعَلُ الْمُتَّقِينَ كَالْفُجَّارِ

Shall We treat those who believe and work deeds of righteousness, the same as those who do mischief on earth? Shall We treat those who guard against evil, the same as those who turn aside from the right?

(Sâd 38:28)

This means 'they are not the same with Us, not in this world or the next', as the Exalted said:

أَمْ حَسِبَ الَّذِينَ اجْتَرَحُوا السَّيِّئَاتِ أَن نَّجْعَلَهُمْ كَالَّذِينَ آمَنُوا وَعَمِلُوا الصَّالِحَاتِ

سَوَاءً مَّحْيَاهُمْ وَمَمَاتُهُمْ سَاءَ مَا يَحْكُمُونَ

What! Do those who seek after evil ways think that We shall hold them equal with those who believe and do righteous deeds, that equal will be their life and their death? Ill is the judgment that they make.

(al-Jâthiya 45:21)

This negates their account and fantasy and faults their judgment, that is, their thought that they and the people of righteousness will be counted the same with their Lord.

Allah has described His angels, prophets and believing servants in His Book as holding fast to righteous deeds and hastening to them with fear, awe, affection and dread. The Exalted said about the angels:

بَلْ عِبَادٌ مُّكْرَمُونَ

لَا يَسْبِقُونَهُ بِالْقَوْلِ وَهُم بِأَمْرِهِ يَعْمَلُونَ

They are (but) servants raised to honour.
They speak not before He speaks,
and they act (in all things) by His Command.
(al-Anbiyâ' 21: 26- 27)

And the Exalted said about the prophets:

أُولَٰئِكَ الَّذِينَ يَدْعُونَ يَبْتَغُونَ إِلَىٰ رَبِّهِمُ الْوَسِيلَةَ أَيُّهُمْ أَقْرَبُ

وَيَرْجُونَ رَحْمَتَهُ وَيَخَافُونَ عَذَابَهُ إِنَّ عَذَابَ رَبِّكَ كَانَ مَحْذُورًا

Those whom they call upon do desire (for themselves) means of access to their Lord, even those who are nearest: they hope for His Mercy and fear His Wrath: for the Wrath of thy Lord is something to take heed of.
(al-Isrâ 17:57)

And He also said:

إِنَّهُمْ كَانُوا يُسَارِعُونَ فِي الْخَيْرَاتِ وَيَدْعُونَنَا رَغَبًا وَرَهَبًا وَكَانُوا لَنَا خَاشِعِينَ

These (three) were ever quick in emulation in good works; they used to call on Us with love and reverence, and humble themselves before Us.
(al-Anbiyâ' 21: 90)

The Exalted said about the believers:

وَلَقَدْ آتَيْنَا مُوسَىٰ وَهَارُونَ الْفُرْقَانَ وَضِيَاءً وَذِكْرًا لِّلْمُتَّقِينَ

الَّذِينَ يَخْشَوْنَ رَبَّهُم بِالْغَيْبِ وَهُم مِّنَ السَّاعَةِ مُشْفِقُونَ

In the past We granted to Moses and Aaron the criterion (for judgment), and a Light and a Message for those who would do right; those who fear their Lord in their most secret thoughts, and who hold the Hour (of Judgment) in awe.
(al-Anbiyâ' 21: 48-49)

And He also said:

إِنَّ الَّذِينَ هُم مِّنْ خَشْيَةِ رَبِّهِم مُّشْفِقُونَ

وَالَّذِينَ هُم بِآيَاتِ رَبِّهِمْ يُؤْمِنُونَ

وَالَّذِينَ هُم بِرَبِّهِمْ لَا يُشْرِكُونَ

وَالَّذِينَ يُؤْتُونَ مَا آتَوا وَّقُلُوبُهُمْ وَجِلَةٌ أَنَّهُمْ إِلَى رَبِّهِمْ رَاجِعُونَ

أُوْلَئِكَ يُسَارِعُونَ فِي الْخَيْرَاتِ وَهُمْ لَهَا سَابِقُونَ

Verily those who live in awe for fear of their Lord; Those who believe in the Signs of their Lord; Those who join not (in worship) partners with their Lord. And those who dispense their charity with their hearts full of fear, because they will return to their Lord; It is these who hasten in every good work, and these who are foremost in them.
(al-Mu'minûn 23:57-61)

When 'Âisha, may Allah be pleased with her, asked the Messenger of Allah, upon him be peace, about the words of the Exalted: '**And those who dispense their charity with their hearts full of fear**,'[56] 'Does it refer to a man who has illicit sex and steals and then fears?' He said: 'No, on the contrary, it is a man who prays and fasts and gives charity and fears that it may not be accepted.'

When Allah described some of His enemies, He attributed delusion and false dreams to them. He said about one of them:

وَمَا أَظُنُّ السَّاعَةَ قَائِمَةً وَلَئِن رُّدِدتُّ إِلَى رَبِّي لَأَجِدَنَّ خَيْرًا مِّنْهَا مُنقَلَبًا

'Nor do I deem that the Hour (of Judgment) will (ever) come: Even if I am brought back to my Lord, I shall surely find (there) something better in exchange.'
(al-Kahf 18:36)

This means his garden which enthralled him and made him forget the blessing of Allah. He took pride in it and held himself in higher esteem than

---

56 al-Mu'minûn 23:60

47

those servants of Allah who were better than him. Look at it in the full story that Allah relates about him and the righteous servant in His Words:

$$وَاضْرِبْ لَهُم مَّثَلًا رَّجُلَيْنِ جَعَلْنَا لِأَحَدِهِمَا جَنَّتَيْنِ مِنْ أَعْنَابٍ$$
$$وَحَفَفْنَاهُمَا بِنَخْلٍ وَجَعَلْنَا بَيْنَهُمَا زَرْعًا$$

Set forth to them the parable of two men: for one of them We provided two gardens of grape-vines and surrounded them with date palms; in between the two We placed corn-fields.
(al-Kahf 18:32)

He said about another of His deluded enemies: '**I shall certainly be given wealth and children**,'[57] meaning in the next world. Allah rejected this claim and promised a punishment would be sent to him.

And the Exalted said about another of them: '**But if I am brought to my Lord, I have good stored in His Sight.**'[58]

Now look – may Allah show you mercy – to the ways Allah described His beloved ones and His friends and at those who displease Him and His enemies. Whichever of the two groups you follow and resemble is the one you will be with. For whoever imitates a people will be among them, as has been related.

It has been made clear to you that the angels of Allah and His prophets and righteous servants hasten towards good and are constant in righteous deeds and avoidance of wrongdoing and transgression and feeling a false sense of security and hopes about Allah. So choose for yourself the company of the better of the two groups. Imitate them in the actions and attributes and you will be among them, *insha'Allah*, God willing.

࿐

Know that hope of forgiveness accompanied by laziness and inactivity are amongst the most dangerous things a person may have. They are rampant on the tongues of those whose states are mixed up. It is for this reason that we stressed this point over and over again in the hope that Allah will benefit the one who reads it and in doing so be stirred from his neglect and woken from his sleep. This will be when he realises that the people of prophethood and righteousness had the most intense fear of Allah to the extent that our Prophet Muhammad, upon him be peace, used to say: 'If Allah were to take me and the son of Mary for what these two have done, referring to his thumb

---

57 Maryam 19: 77.
58 al-Fussilat 41:50.

and index finger, he would punish us and that would not be an injustice.'[59] There is no doubt that the prophets and saints are more knowledgeable of Allah and of His enormous generosity and expansive mercy than anyone else. And it remains that the people of mixed up states and shortcomings should be more fearful in all circumstances than them.

꙳

Know that the arguments of those deluded by false hope can be proved wrong with very little effort. If he says, 'Allah, the Exalted, cannot be harmed by our sin and does not benefit from our obedience. He is beyond me and my actions', tell him, 'you have spoken the truth, but your sins harm you and your acts of obedience benefit you. You are in need of righteous deeds.' Then you should say to him, 'why don't you give up on earning and movement and exertion for a living, for surely the Exalted has guaranteed provision for you and the treasures of the heavens and earth are in His grasp.' He is likely to say to you, 'that is true, but exertion and movement is necessary because it is very rare that we see something happen without them.' And so say to him, 'if this world, which Allah has ordered you to abstain from and forbade you from desiring and of which He apportioned that which will suffice you, only comes through seeking it and making an effort, and the next world, to which Allah exhorted us and which He commanded us to seek and about which He informed you in His Book upon the tongue of His Prophet that you will not be saved in it from His punishment or successful in His rewards unless you strive and work hard for it, yet we still see you lax and uncaring about it, then you are nothing but one full of doubt or a deluded fool. The situation has been turned upside down. You have placed things in their wrong place. In what manner are you to meet Allah and how will you meet His Messenger, upon him be peace, whom He sent to call you from the temporal world to the everlasting world?' With that, his argument will be defeated and he will not know what he says.

꙳

Know – may Allah have mercy on you – with certainty, that whenever faith gets stronger and the deeds more righteous, fear becomes greater. Whenever faith becomes weaker and actions worse, fear becomes less and false security and delusion become more overwhelming. Examine that in yourself and others and it will become clear.

In summary, the true believer is one who does righteous actions and is

59   Related by Abu Nu'aym in *al-Hilya* on the authority of Abû Hurairah.

sincere in them, hoping for acceptance and reward from Allah's bounty. He stays away and distances himself from wickedness. He fears being tested by them. He is in awe of retribution for what he has done and hopes for forgiveness from Allah after repenting and turning to Allah. Any of the believers who does not have these attributes is one of the *mukhalatin*, those whose states are mixed up. He is in grave danger. Understand this summary and examine yourself by it and you will be successful and safe, *insha'Allah*, God willing.

A sign of felicity is that Allah enables the servant to perform righteous acts and makes them easy during his lifetime. A sign of wretchedness is that righteous acts are not easy for him and he is tested by wicked deeds. The Messenger of Allah, upon him be peace, said: 'Act, for everyone will find easy that for which he was created. Whoever was created for the Garden will find easy the actions of the people of the Garden. And whoever was created for the Fire will find easy the acts of the people of the Fire.'[60] When Allah grasped the two handfuls, He said to the handful of the people of felicity, 'these are the people of the Garden and they will do the acts of the people of the Garden'. And He said to the handful of the people of wretchedness, 'these are for the Fire and they will do the acts of the people of the Fire.'

Know that the believer who has insight into the religion and who is firm in knowledge and certainty is one who excels in his actions. He gives his whole being and then he relies upon Allah and His bounty and does not rely on his actions and his excellence. This is the attribute of the prophets, the righteous scholars and virtuous early and later generations, upon them be salutations, mercy and satisfaction.

This is what the Messenger, upon him be peace, indicated in his statement: 'No one enters the Garden by his actions.' They said, 'not even you O Messenger of Allah.' He said: 'Not even I, it is only that Allah encompassed me with His mercy[61].' This statement should be taken in the context that he, upon him be peace, used to go to the utmost limit and degree to the extent that his heels would swell up because of the length of his standing in prayer.

As for someone who acts righteously but then depends on his own actions, he is self-glorifying and daring towards his Lord. He might be tested to expose his inability and the lack of ability to act righteously if it were not for the bounties and mercy of Allah, as the Exalted said:

$$وَلَوْ لَا فَضْلُ اللَّهِ عَلَيْكُمْ وَرَحْمَتُهُ مَا زَكَا مِنكُم مِّنْ أَحَدٍ أَبَدًا$$

60   Related by Abû Hanifa in his *Musnad* on the authority of Sa'd.
61   Related by al-Bukhâri in *The Book of Subtleties* (*al-Riqâq*) (*hadîth* number 6099) and Muslim in *The Book of The Description of the Resurrection, the Garden and the Fire* (*hadîth* number 2816).

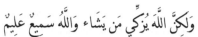

And were it not for the grace and mercy of Allah on you, not one of you would ever have been pure: but Allah doth purify whom He pleases: and Allah is One Who hears and knows (all things).

(al-Nûr 24:21)

It reached us concerning the Day of Judgement that a servant worshipped Allah for five hundred years. Allah will say to him, 'O my servant, enter my Garden by My mercy.' He will say, 'O Lord, by my actions!' At this, Allah will order to take all his actions to account and measure them against the blessing of sight. All his worship was exhausted and there remained many blessings that still needed to be accounted for and as a result he was ordered to be taken to the Fire. At this he said, 'O Lord, enter me into Your Garden by Your mercy.' He ordered him to be taken to it and he praised and thanked Him, Majestic and High is He. From this, two things are clear. The first of them is the need for righteous actions. The second is the need for dependence on Allah and no one or thing else.

How excellent are the words of the Reviver of the Religion, Abdul Qâdir al-Jaylâni[62], may Allah be pleased with him, when he said: 'To You, we cannot arrive; yet, without You, we cannot either.' The meaning of this statement is that we cannot arrive by our actions. It is only by the bounty of Allah. However, we must still do the actions to fulfil the commands of Allah.

Abu Saîd al-Kharrâz[63], may Allah the Exalted show him mercy, said: 'Whoever imagines he can arrive by his actions is one in drudgery (*Muta'anin*). Whoever imagines he can arrive without action is one living in false hopes (*Mutamanin*).' One who lives in false hope is one who does nothing but imagines that he is depending on the generosity of Allah. That is self delusion and idiocy. It is only correct that he depends on Allah and on His generosity if he acts righteously, as already presented.

Hasan al-Basri[64], Allah's mercy be upon him, said: 'False hopes of forgiveness have played with many a group of people and as a result, they left the world bankrupt'. This means 'bankrupt of any good actions.'

He also said: 'A believer gathers goodness and fear whereas a hypocrite gathers wickedness and a false sense of security.'

I said: This is extremely strange as fear is more appropriate for a wicked

---

62 Abdul Qâdir al-Jaylâni was a scholar and spiritual master to whom the Qâdiri spiritual path is attributed. He died in Baghdad in 561H/ 1166 CE.

63 Abu Saîd, Ahmed ibn 'Isa al-Kharrâz was an early scholar famous for his sublime sayings and allegories. He died in 285H/ 899 CE.

64 Hasan al-Basri was born in Madina and was raised under the supervision of 'Ali ibn Abi Tâlib. He became the Imâm of Basra and was known as the 'Crown of the Followers.' He died in Basra in 110H/ 728 CE.

person due to his exposure by his wickedness to Allah's power. He only has the false sense of security because his heart is inverted and his inner eye is blind. However, 'he whom Allah leaves to stray, for him will you find no protector to lead him to the Right Way.'[65]

O Allah guide us and be with us, O our Lord, and be a friend and protector who guides to that which you love and pleases You. For we have entrusted our affairs to You. Let us die as Muslims and gather us with the righteous.

BELIEF IN PREDETERMINATION AND DESTINY

The argument of blaming predestination, which the Devil causes to flow from the tongues of many of the Muslims, is extremely dangerous. This is when it is said to one of them who has neglected some obligations or performed some forbidden acts, 'why have you done that which contradicts the orders of Allah and His Messenger?' They say, 'it was already predetermined, destined and written for me.' By saying this, he excuses himself and lifts the responsibility from himself and argues against Allah the Exalted. He has a clear argument against all His creation in every state for '**He cannot be questioned for His acts but they will be asked.**'[66]

I say: The statement of this disobedient person is greater and more dangerous in both worlds than his act of disobedience. This is because the meaning of this statement demonstrates that the inner belief in the pillars of the faith of the one who said it is shaky at its very foundation. When will this disobedient person repent? When will he regret his ugly acts? When will he ask forgiveness for them? He does not see that he has performed them and claims that he was forced and compelled into it and that he has no choice or power. This is in reality the belief of the Jabariyya Sect.[67] They were a group of innovators. They argued that we have no free will. They were the exact opposite of the Mutazila sect who were another people of innovation. The belief of the people of truth, the People of the Prophetic Way and the Congregation (*ahl al-Sunnah wa'l-Jama'a*) is the middle way between these two groups. They are, as some scholars have said, like the milk that flows from between blood and excrement yet is pure and agreeable to those who drink it.

---

65 Al-Kahf 17:18.
66 Al-Anbiyâ 21:23.
67 The Jabariyya sect, also known as the Jahmiyya, introduced several false notions into Islam. They denied many of the divine attributes and believed that humans were compelled into action with no choice or will. It was founded by Jahm ibn Safwan who was executed as a heretic in 128H/ 745 CE.

The belief of the People of the Prophetic Way (*ahl al-Sunnah*), may Allah make us from amongst them by His bounty, is that no occurrence however small or great occurs except by the determination (*qadâ*) of the Exalted and by His Bearing (*mashîya*), His Will (*irâda*) and His Power (*qudra*). All servants and their actions, the good thereof and the bad, are the creation of Allah the Exalted. After that, they have been required to fulfil all the commands of Allah and they have not been granted license to omit any of them. They are responsible for not falling into forbidden things and are expected to avoid them totally. If they fall into some aspect of them, they hasten to Allah with repentance and the asking of forgiveness. If they fall short in fulfilling some aspects of the commands, they hasten to complete them and repent to Allah the Exalted for what they abandoned. They would never argue in favour of themselves against Allah and would not use predestination as an excuse. Nor would they offer licence for someone else to do that. For surely Allah the Exalted has described some of His enemies in His Book as justifying themselves by way of claiming divine predetermination. After mentioning them, He rebukes them and rejects their claims. He does not accept it from them, rejects it and denies them. The Exalted has said:

سَيَقُولُ الَّذِينَ أَشْرَكُواْ لَوْ شَاءَ اللّهُ مَا أَشْرَكْنَا وَلاَ آبَاؤُنَا وَلاَ حَرَّمْنَا مِن شَيْءٍ

كَذَلِكَ كَذَّبَ الَّذِينَ مِن قَبْلِهِم حَتَّى ذَاقُواْ بَأْسَنَا قُلْ هَلْ عِندَكُم مِّنْ عِلْمٍ فَتُخْرِجُوهُ لَنَا

إِن تَتَّبِعُونَ إِلاَّ الظَّنَّ وَإِنْ أَنتُمْ إِلاَّ تَخْرُصُونَ

قُلْ فَلِلّهِ الْحُجَّةُ الْبَالِغَةُ

Those who give partners (to Allah. will say: "If Allah had wished, we should not have given partners to Him nor would our fathers; nor should we have had any taboos." So did their ancestors argue falsely, until they tasted of Our wrath." Say: "Have you any (certain) knowledge? If so, produce it before us. You follow nothing but conjecture: you do nothing but lie. Say: "With Allah is the argument that reaches home".'
(al-Anâm 6:148-149)

And in another verse:

وَقَالَ الَّذِينَ أَشْرَكُواْ لَوْ شَاءَ اللّهُ مَا عَبَدْنَا مِن دُونِهِ مِن شَيْءٍ نَّحْنُ وَلاَ آبَاؤُنَا وَلاَ

حَرَّمْنَا مِن دُونِهِ مِن شَيْءٍ كَذَلِكَ فَعَلَ الَّذِينَ مِن قَبْلِهِمْ فَهَلْ عَلَى الرُّسُلِ إِلاَّ الْبَلاغُ الْمُبِينُ

The worshippers of false gods say: "If Allah had so willed, we should not have worshipped aught but Him – neither we nor our fathers, nor should we have prescribed prohibitions other than His." So did those who went before them. But what is the mission of apostles but to preach the Clear Message?

(al-Nahl 16:35)

So beware of following the polytheists in their arguing against Allah, Lord of the Worlds. It should suffice you to believe in predetermination, the good thereof and the bad. Then you should compel yourself to fulfil Allah's commands and to avoid His prohibitions. Repent to Him from all your shortcomings in fulfilling His rights – Exalted is He! And seek help from Allah, the Exalted. Depend on Him. Indeed, he, upon whom be salutations and peace, said: 'If predetermination is mentioned then abstain.'[68] This is a prohibition from entering into (detailed discussions about) it because of the inherent dangers and many potential harms.

A man asked 'Ali, may Allah be pleased with him, about predetermination. He answered: 'It is a deep ocean, so do not enter it. It is a dark road, so do not travel it. It is one of Allah's secrets, so do not delve into it.'

One of the men of authority asked Muhammad bin Wâsi, may Allah show him mercy, about predetermination. He said to him: Your neighbour is one of the inhabitants of the grave. Reflection on that should occupy you, not predetermination. The practice of the early and later generations of the people of true belief was to believe in predetermination, the good and bad thereof. They were unanimous upon that – may Allah show them mercy. Likewise, they were united in holding back from justification of neglecting commands and entering into the forbidden through arguing predetermination and destiny. If you are one of the people of truth – follow them! Travel their path. And if you do not, then you have heard the words of Allah the Exalted to those who travelled a path that differed from the way of the believers. Allah the Exalted said:

وَمَن يُشَاقِقِ الرَّسُولَ مِن بَعْدِ مَا تَبَيَّنَ لَهُ الْهُدَى وَيَتَّبِعْ غَيْرَ سَبِيلِ الْمُؤْمِنِينَ نُوَلِّهِ مَا تَوَلَّى وَنُصْلِهِ جَهَنَّمَ وَسَاءَتْ مَصِيرًا

If anyone contends with the Messenger even after guidance has been plainly conveyed to him, and follows a path other than that becoming to men of Faith, We shall leave him in the path he has chosen, and land him in Hell – what an evil refuge!

(al-Nisâ 4:115)

68 Related by al-Tabarâni on the authority of Ibn Masûd.

54

Then know – may Allah show you mercy – that it is not permitted and not correct for you to believe within yourself that there is no blemish or fault upon him for abandoning a compulsion or doing something forbidden because destiny has overwhelmed and overtaken him. If, based on this, he does something or omits something that Allah is not pleased with and then pleads predetermination as his excuse while he still in fact has choice and free will, then, indeed, he is proposing a falsehood and carrying a flagrant sin.

I fear that this affliction has crept into the thinking of people associated with knowledge and virtue, not to mention the general populace of Muslims. Among the things that suggest this is the lack of abundant pain, hurt and regret when they act in ways which are considered reproachable and offensive in the Islamic legal system. A believer who feels this within himself should fear Allah and strive to remove it from himself. He should know that Allah will not excuse him because of predetermination nor will He accept his justification as long as he had choice. So if you hear any Muslim presenting this false justification, you should admonish him. Inform him that the sin of justifying his wrongdoing by arguing predetermination and destiny is greater than his abandonment of a command or doing a prohibited action and so he should fear Allah and that he should not carry upon himself two afflictions that drive him to the wrath of Allah from two directions.

As for mentioning predetermination and destiny and reminding oneself about it in times of difficulties, calamities and misfortunes, there is no problem in that. It is a proposition that helps oneself and does not justify one's self (and its bad actions). The servant who is undergoing tribulation and misfortune knows that the One who is testing him is his Lord, the Merciful One and that the calamity has already been predetermined by Allah the Exalted. He realises and attains certainty that in what has happened there is much good and benefit. This knowledge leads him to satisfaction with and submission to Allah, the all-Wise and all-Knowing. It has already been made clear and expounded that pleading destiny for commands and prohibitions is dangerous and blameworthy so beware, but at times of calamity it is beneficial but only for one who is mindful of Allah. Allah the Exalted said:

$$\text{مَا أَصَابَ مِن مُّصِيبَةٍ فِي الْأَرْضِ وَلَا فِي أَنفُسِكُمْ إِلَّا فِي كِتَابٍ مِّن قَبْلِ أَن نَّبْرَأَهَا}$$

$$\text{إِنَّ ذَٰلِكَ عَلَى اللَّهِ يَسِيرٌ}$$

$$\text{لِّكَيْلَا تَأْسَوْا عَلَىٰ مَا فَاتَكُمْ وَلَا تَفْرَحُوا بِمَا آتَاكُمْ وَاللَّهُ لَا يُحِبُّ كُلَّ مُخْتَالٍ فَخُورٍ}$$

'No misfortune can happen on earth or in your souls but is recorded in a decree before We bring it into existence: That is truly easy for Allah. In

order that ye may not despair over matters that pass you by, or exult over favours bestowed upon you. For Allah loves not any vain glorious boaster.
(al-Hadîd 57:22-23)

If the servant mentions at times of calamity and misfortune that Allah has promised ranks and rewards, this would be good. This is beneficial to most Muslims and easy for them to comprehend. This is because delving into the issue of pre-existent knowledge, destiny and predetermination requires wisdom and insight that only a few people possess, whereas the other worldly rewards are understood by everyone. This is also true of threats of punishment. Because of this, reminding of the promises and threats is generally beneficial at times of trial, in obedience and in disobedience. For this reason, you can see that the Book of Allah and tradition of His Messenger, upon him be peace, are full of promises and threats and warnings and reminders. Understand this. Contemplate it and be guided by it. Depend upon Allah, for surely Allah loves those who depend on Him. There is no power or ability except by Allah, the High and the Mighty.

‍⁌⁍

DISCOURSE ON
KNOWLEDGE

NOW, O BROTHERS, may Allah endow us and you with a state of well being
and certainty and take us and you along the path of the righteous
ones (*al-Muttaqîn*) that every Muslim, male and female, must be aware
of *Ilm*, sacred knowledge. There is no excuse for any Muslim ever to abandon
it. That is, the *ilm*, sacred knowledge, without which one's faith and Islam are
not correct. In summary, it is 'knowledge of Allah and His Messengers and
the Last Day; the knowledge of what Allah has prescribed as compulsions
and the forbidden things that He has prescribed we leave'. For certainly, the
Messenger of Allah, upon him be peace, has said: 'Seeking knowledge is a
compulsion upon every Muslim'.[1] And he, upon him be peace, has said: 'Seek
knowledge even it be in China'.[2] China is a region in one of the most distant
places. Few people will ever reach it because of its distance. Therefore, if it
is necessary for the Muslim to seek knowledge even in this distant land, how
can it not be a compulsion upon him if he is among scholars and where there
is no hardship or difficulty to be found in acquiring it?

The sciences of Islam are based upon the words of the Messenger, upon
him be peace. When asked by the angel Gabriel, who said, 'tell me about
Islam'; he, upon him be peace, replied, 'Islam is to bear witness that there is
no god but Allah and that Muhammad is the Messenger of Allah, to establish
the prayer, to give the *zakât*, to fast the month of Ramadân and to perform
the pilgrimage to the House for whoever is able.' He then said, 'tell me about
al-Imân, faith.' He, upon him be peace, said, '*al-Imân* is to believe in Allah,
His angels, His books, His Messengers, the Last Day and destiny, the good

---

1   Related by Ibn Mâjah (*hadîth* number 224).
2   Related by al-Bayhaqi in *al-Madkhal* and the *Branches of Faith* and by Ibn Abdul Barr in *Jami
Bayân al-'Ilm* on the authority of Anas ibn Mâlik.

thereof and the bad.' The *hadîth* is a long one.[3]

As for the science of *Imân*, belief, there are summarised creeds compiled by the scholars for the general populace of Muslims. The creed of Imâm al-Ghazâli is one such example. It is comprehensive and beneficial and contains some extra matters that are necessary for the believer to consolidate, strengthen and perfect his or her faith. [We will relate at the end of this text, if Allah wills 'the simplified creed that encompasses the knowledge of *Imân* that must be known'].

The sciences of Islam are found in the writings of the scholars and jurists, may Allah be pleased with them. The necessary amount for an individual is that which he or she is not allowed to be ignorant of. For example, knowing about the compulsion of the five daily prayers, how they are performed, their conditions, their timings, the purification associated with them and such matters. It would include the knowledge of the compulsion of *zakât*, alms purification, its amount and its timing. Likewise, knowledge of the fast of Ramadân, its prerequisites and the things which annul it, and knowledge of the compulsion of the pilgrimage for one who is able and the conditions that make one 'able'.

In summary, it is necessary for the Muslim to know the individual obligations and the forbidden acts, of which knowledge aims to prevent one from falling into, such as adultery, homosexuality, the consumption of intoxicants, the unjust treatment of people, theft, fraud, lying, backbiting, slander and so forth.

Knowledge of the specific rulings of *zakât* is not an obligation upon someone who has no wealth. Likewise knowledge of the essential elements and conditions of the pilgrimage is not obligatory upon someone who is unable to perform it. It is only compulsory at the point he determines to travel or he is about to perform it. As for the knowledge of the general obligation to perform Hajj and to pay *zakât*, this is an obligation upon every Muslim.

Regarding the knowledge of the conditions of buying and selling, general transactions and marriage, it is obligatory to know Allah's rulings regarding these things when one intends to embark upon them. He or she should know what makes them sound and what invalidates them, from the outset and throughout. He must know this, otherwise he may encounter, willingly or unwillingly, Allah's wrath. For indeed, the ignorant one, through his ignorance, exposes himself to Allah's anger and risks destruction in every state. And how could that not be the case? Perhaps, he may mistakenly believe that some of the compulsions are not compulsory or even that they are forbidden or that some of the forbidden acts are not forbidden or are actually compulsions or acts of obedience. This is the utmost danger and

---

3   Related by Muslim in the *Book of Faith* (*hadîth* number 8).

potential harm for the ignorant one. Perhaps he may fall into things which resemble disbelief or are actually disbelief, as anyone who ponders this state and reflects upon their words and actions will realise. Allah will not excuse him. He – Exalted be He – has obliged them to seek knowledge and facilitated the means for it and obligated the scholars to teach them. Therefore, their shortcomings are purely because of their own preoccupation with the temporal world and the following of their own desires, which only increases their distance from Allah and His abhorrence and rejection.

It is amazing to see how the ignorant one, preoccupied by self deception, is tireless in his pursuit of the world, day and night. His greed for it does not cease. He has great concern for amassing it and keeping others away from it. He finds many excuses for this behaviour, yet he is ignorant of the affairs of his religion, does not seek sacred knowledge and has never sat with a scholar to learn from him. When it is pointed out to him, he justifies himself in a way that has no value in Allah's eyes, citing lack of time and having too many preoccupations. This is despite the fact that, Allah, may He be praised, had made the pursuit of knowledge easy for him by providing scholars and that there are very few barriers to learning essential knowledge. The temporal affairs are the opposite of this. One hardly achieves any small portion of it without difficulty and great effort. This (state of finding seeking knowledge difficult while pursuing the temporal world) is purely a result of the death of the heart. A person's concern for the world and lack of celebration of the affairs of the next world are because he only sees the immediate and apparent needs and considers his need for knowledge as extremely distant, as he does not need it and will not know its benefit until after death. He has forgotten death and what follows it as a result of being overwhelmed by ignorance and lack of knowledge.

The one possessing these attributes is among those about whom Allah says:

$$يَعْلَمُونَ ظَاهِرًا مِّنَ الْحَيَاةِ الدُّنْيَا وَهُمْ عَنِ الْآخِرَةِ هُمْ غَافِلُونَ$$

They know but the outer (things) in the life of this world: but of the end of things they are heedless.
(Rûm 30:7)

Hasan al-Basri, may Allah show him mercy, said that one of them is able to take a dirham on his finger tip and tell you its weight because of his deep knowledge of worldly affairs, yet if he were asked about the preconditions of purification or prayer he would not know.

In summary, ignorance is the head of all evil and tribulations in this world and the next. If all the enemies of the ignorant one were to gather against him, they would not be able to harm him as much as he has already harmed himself, as the poet has said:

مَا يَبْلُغُ الْأَعْدَاءُ مِنْ جَاهِلٍ   مَا يَبْلُغُ الْجَاهِلُ مِنْ نَفْسِه

The enemies of the ignorant one will reach not
What the ignorant one himself reaches

And another has said:

و في الْجُهْلِ قَبْلَ الْمَوتِ مَوْتٌ لِأَهْلِه   فَأَجْسَادُهُمْ قَبْلَ الْقُبُورِ قُبُورُ

In ignorance there is death before death for its possessor
Their bodies are graves before their graves.

Ignorance of the sacred knowledge that Allah has obliged one to learn, is blameworthy in all respects. Safeguard yourself, O brother, from it. Leave the darkness of ignorance for the light of knowledge. You do not have to become an expert, just know the amount you are obliged to study and that you need and cannot do without.

Just as you must learn, you must also teach your family, children and all of those who are under your responsibility. If you are unable to teach them yourself, you must order them to go to the people of knowledge, until they learn all that is obligatory upon them. Otherwise, you would have sinned and those among them who are legally responsible (*mukallaf*) would have sinned.

The amount of knowledge that is obligatory upon every Muslim is not much. Its acquisition will hardly entail any difficulty for the seeker, by the Will of Allah, as Allah assists and facilitates the one whose intention is sound. He will receive an immense reward.

The Messenger of Allah, upon him be peace, said: 'One who travels a path seeking sacred knowledge, Allah will make easy for him the path to the Garden.'[4] And he, upon him be peace, said: 'The angels lower their wings for the seeker of sacred knowledge, pleased with what he is doing.'[5] And he, upon him be peace, said: 'Attending the gatherings of sacred knowledge is greater than the performance of a thousand prayer cycles, visiting a thousand sick

---

4   Related by Abû Dawûd (*hadîth* number 3637).

5   Related with this wording by al-Tayâlasi on the authority of Safwân. However, the various narrations which are synonymous including the one quoted above and al-Tirmidhi *hadîth* number 2752 and 3671.

people, and attending a thousand funerals.'⁶ And he, upon him be peace, said, 'Allah undertakes responsibility for the sustenance of the seeker of knowledge.' This responsibility is a special responsibility beyond His general responsibility for all creatures on the earth as expressed in His words

$$ \text{وَمَا مِن دَابَّةٍ فِي الأَرْضِ إِلاَّ عَلَى اللَّهِ رِزْقُهَا} $$

There is not a creature on the earth but that Allah bears its sustenance.
(Hud 11:6)

Its meaning is 'increase in ease and removal of hardships in the seeking and acquiring provision'. And Allah knows best.

In a long *hadîth*, the Messenger, upon him be peace, said, 'it, that is, sacred knowledge, is inspired in the felicitous and prevented from the wretched.'

As you already know from what we have presented, there is no excuse for the ignorant one to neglect the pursuit of knowledge, likewise, there is no excuse for the knowledgeable one to neglect practising it.

The ignorant one that falls short in seeking the required knowledge is like a servant who has been sent a book from his master that contains injunctions and prohibitions. The servant does not even look at the book nor does he know what it contains despite his ability and capacity to become well acquainted with it. One who has knowledge without action is like he who looks at the book of his master and has knowledge of its information but does not comply with its injunctions nor refrains from its prohibitions. So reflect, may Allah have mercy on you! Have you seen negligence more appalling than the failure of these two servants to uphold the right of their master? Would you be able to provide an excuse or justification for them? Is there anyone more deserving of punitive and exemplary punishment (*al-i'qâb wal-nikâl*) than these two for their disobedience and lack of respect for their master? Then, beware of being one of these two unfortunate men, the ignorant one that does not learn and the knowledgeable one who does not act upon his knowledge. You will perish and lose out in this world and the next and indeed that is a clear loss.

As for the broadening of one's beneficial religious knowledge and excelling in it and going beyond one's actual needs, this is one of the main means towards Allah and one of the most excellent virtues with Him. But this is only if studying is sincere and is purely for seeking the Countenance of Allah and accompanied by a demand upon oneself to apply and teach the knowledge to other slaves of Allah, only hoping for the Countenance of Allah and the abode of the Hereafter.

This is the rank that comes immediately after the rank of prophethood

6   Mentioned as a *khabr*, tradition, by al-Munawi in his *Fayd al-Qadîr* when commenting on *hadîth* number 1831.

and all the other ranks of the believers follow. The scholars that embody their knowledge are the medium between the Messenger of Allah, upon him be peace, and the Muslims. Allah has said in reference to the excellence of the scholars:

$$\text{شَهِدَ اللّٰهُ أَنَّهُ لَا إِلَهَ إِلَّا هُوَ وَالْمَلَائِكَةُ وَأُولُوا الْعِلْمِ قَائِمًا بِالْقِسْطِ}$$

$$\text{لَا إِلَهَ إِلَّا هُوَ الْعَزِيزُ الْحَكِيمُ}$$

Allah bears witness that there is no god but Him, as do the angels and the people of knowledge, upholding justice.
(âli Imrân 3:18)

Notice how they have been linked with His angels in bearing witness to His Oneness and His justice.

Allah, Exalted be He, said:

$$\text{قُلْ هَلْ يَسْتَوِي الَّذِينَ يَعْلَمُونَ وَالَّذِينَ لَا يَعْلَمُونَ}$$

Say, are they the same – those who know and those who do not know?
(al-Zumar 39:9)

They are not equal either in the temporal world nor the Hereafter, rather Allah has preferred the people of knowledge over those who do not know by many degrees, as He, Exalted be He, has said:

$$\text{يَرْفَعِ اللّٰهُ الَّذِينَ آمَنُوا مِنكُمْ وَالَّذِينَ أُوتُوا الْعِلْمَ دَرَجَاتٍ وَاللّٰهُ بِمَا تَعْمَلُونَ خَبِيرٌ}$$

Allah will raise in rank those of you who believe and those that have been given knowledge.
(al-Mujâdalah 58:11)

What is meant here is that those who have knowledge will be raised above those who believe (but do not have knowledge).

And he, upon him be peace and salutations, said: 'The scholars are the inheritors of the prophets because the prophets do not bequeath gold and silver coins rather they bequeath knowledge.'[7]

And he, upon him be peace and salutations, said: 'There is no envy except in two cases – a man whom Allah has granted wisdom and he judges by it and teaches it day and night and a man whom Allah has given wealth and he spends it day and night.'[8] The meaning of 'envy' here is 'al-ghibta' (which

---

7   Related by al-Tirmidhî (*hadîth* number 2858), Abû Dawûd (*hadîth* number 3641) and Ibn Mâjah (*hadîth* number 223).

8   Related by al-Bukhâri in *The Book of Monotheism* (al-Tawhîd) (*hadîth* number 8091) and

is a positive feeling of aspiring to acquire a quality without wanting it to be taken from the other person) and it is praiseworthy with regard to affairs of the next world.

The Messenger of Allah, upon him be peace, said: 'The preference of the scholar over the worshipper (*âbid*) is like my preference over the lowest of my companions.'[9] In another version, it has been said 'like the moon on the night when it is full over the rest of the planets.'[10] If the preference of the scholar amounts to this when compared to the worshipper who is not devoid of knowledge as he could not really be a worshipper if he had no knowledge of worship, then what is his preference compared to the man of ignorance?

The merits of knowledge and those that possess it are countless. They are well documented in the Book of Allah, the tradition (*sunnah*) of His Messenger, upon him be peace, and the tradition of the righteous predecessors. Many books are filled with the virtues of knowledge and of the scholars. Ali, may Allah be pleased with him, used to say, 'knowledge is better than wealth since knowledge protects you while you protect wealth. Knowledge increases when you share it, while wealth decreases. Knowledge is a judge while wealth is judged over.'

৵৹

Know that the scholar who does not act upon his knowledge is stripped of this preferential status. He should not be misled by what has been mentioned by Allah and his Messenger, upon him be peace, regarding the excellence of knowledge and delude himself into thinking that he is included in that solely by knowledge without action. The Messenger of Allah, upon him be peace, said, 'learn what you will, for, by Allah, it will not be accepted from you until you act upon it.'[11] And he, upon him be peace, said, 'one who increases in knowledge and does not increase in guidance increases in nothing but distance from Allah.'[12] Knowledge only gains that high rank with Allah when it benefits the servants of Allah. When a scholar does not derive benefit from his knowledge, how can others derive benefit from it? So recognise the loss of excellence that will befall one who has knowledge but does not act upon it. The Messenger, upon him be peace, said: 'The person most severely punished on the Day of Judgement will be the scholar whom Allah did not benefit

Muslim in *The Book of the Prayer of the Traveller* (*hadîth* number 266).
9   Related by al-Tirmidhî (*hadîth* number 2826).
10   Related by Abû Dawûd (*hadîth* number 3637) and Ibn Mâjah (*hadîth* number 223).
11   Related by Ibn Asâkir on the authority of Abû Dardâ and Ibn Abdul Barr and al-Dârimi with the wording, 'learn what you wish for Allah will not benefit you by it unless you act upon it.'
12   Related with this wording by al-Daylami on the authority of 'Ali ibn Abi Tâlib.

by his knowledge.'[13] For that reason, the Messenger of Allah, upon him be peace, used to seek refuge from knowledge that does not benefit and from a heart that does not feel humility. The scholar that does not act upon his knowledge has nothing but the empty shell and mere image of knowledge devoid of its true meaning and reality. Some of the righteous predecessors may Allah's mercy be upon them, said, 'knowledge invites to action. Either he answers or it leaves,' meaning 'its spirit, light and blessing goes and only the outer form remains. This does not go, but rather stays as evidence against the blameworthy scholar.'

On the other hand, if this scholar teaches his knowledge to people and they derive benefit from him, then he is like a burning candle that illuminates for the people or a needle that sews the clothes of the naked. Allah, Exalted be He, has said:

أَتَأْمُرُونَ النَّاسَ بِالْبِرِّ وَتَنْسَوْنَ أَنْفُسَكُمْ وَأَنْتُمْ تَتْلُونَ الْكِتَابَ أَفَلَا تَعْقِلُونَ

Do you order people to devoutness and forget yourselves when you recite the Book, will you not use your intellects?
(al-Baqara 2:44)

And in a *hadîth*, it is related that 'the scholar will be called to the Fire with his entrails pulled out and he will circulate among the people in the Fire as the donkey circulates around the millstone. The people of the Fire will surround him and ask, "what is your situation?" He will reply, "I used to command the good and not act upon it and I would forbid the wrong but commit it myself."'[14]

The scholar who teaches people but does not act upon it is at a loss and is in great danger. However, his state is better than one who does not act or teach the people. He is indeed in loss in every respect and is ruined in every state since he possesses no good and provides no benefit at all. It is feared that he will be among those about whom the Messenger, upon him be peace, said: 'A group of the bearers of Quran will be brought to the Fire before the idol worshippers. They will say "do you precede with us prior to the idol worshippers?" It will be said to them, "yes, one who knows is not the same as one that does not know."'[15]

This scholar, by not acting on his knowledge nor teaching others, inevitably calls to evil, opens for the common folk doors to false interpretations and

---

13   Related by al-Tabarâni in *al-Saghîr* and al-Bayhaqi in the *Branches of Faith* on the authority of Abû Hurairah.

14   Related by al-Bukhâri in *The Book of the Description of the Fire* (*hadîth* number 3094) and Muslim in *The Book of the Abstinence and Subtleties* (*hadîth* number 2989).

15   Related by al-Tabarâni in *al-Kabîr* on the authority of Musâ ibn Muhammad.

license and allows them to be deceived and misled in their duties towards each other and thus to the violation of rights. He is a deviant devil, an evildoer setting himself up in animosity against Allah and His Messenger. Satan has taken him as his representative and a deputy in spreading mischief, error and misguidance. With Allah, he is amongst those that have been described as donkeys and dogs in depravity and disgrace. In fact, donkeys and dogs are better than him as they end up as soil and dust while he ends up in the Fire. Allah, Exalted be He, has said:

$$مَثَلُ الَّذِينَ حُمِّلُوا التَّوْرَاةَ ثُمَّ لَمْ يَحْمِلُوهَا كَمَثَلِ الْحِمَارِ يَحْمِلُ أَسْفَارًا$$

$$بِئْسَ مَثَلُ الْقَوْمِ الَّذِينَ كَذَّبُوا بِآيَاتِ اللَّهِ وَاللَّهُ لَا يَهْدِي الْقَوْمَ الظَّالِمِينَ$$

**The likes of those that were charged with the Torah, but then have
not upheld it, is that of a donkey loaded with weighty tomes, how evil is
the example of those who deny Allah's signs. Allah does not guide the
wrongdoers.'**
(al-Jumah 62:5)

And:

$$وَاتْلُ عَلَيْهِمْ نَبَأَ الَّذِي آتَيْنَاهُ آيَاتِنَا فَانسَلَخَ مِنْهَا فَأَتْبَعَهُ الشَّيْطَانُ فَكَانَ مِنَ الْغَاوِينَ$$

$$وَلَوْ شِئْنَا لَرَفَعْنَاهُ بِهَا وَلَكِنَّهُ أَخْلَدَ إِلَى الْأَرْضِ وَاتَّبَعَ هَوَاهُ$$

$$فَمَثَلُهُ كَمَثَلِ الْكَلْبِ إِن تَحْمِلْ عَلَيْهِ يَلْهَثْ أَوْ تَتْرُكْهُ يَلْهَث$$

$$ذَّلِكَ مَثَلُ الْقَوْمِ الَّذِينَ كَذَّبُوا بِآيَاتِنَا فَاقْصُصِ الْقَصَصَ لَعَلَّهُمْ يَتَفَكَّرُونَ$$

**Relate to them the story of the man to whom We sent Our signs, but he
passed them by: so Satan followed him up, and he went astray.
If it had been Our will, We should have elevated him with Our signs;
but he inclined to the earth, and followed his own vain desires. His
similitude is that of a dog: if you attack him, he lolls out his tongue, or if
you leave him alone, he (still) lolls out his tongue. That is the similitude
of those who reject Our signs; So relate the story; perchance they may
reflect.**
(al-Arâf 7:175-176)

Umar, may Allah be pleased with him, used to say, 'the thing I fear most for you is a hypocrite with a knowledgeable tongue'. For the like of this corrupt hypocrite who has outward knowledge of the Book and the Tradition (*sunnah*) will be greater tribulation and mischief for the Muslims. The Messenger of Allah, upon him be peace, said of such people, 'there is something I am more afraid of for you than the antichrist (*al-Dajjâl*).' They asked, 'and what is that?' He, upon him be peace, said, 'evil scholars'.[16] He described a group of people who read the Quran but it does not go beyond their throats (that is, they pay it mere lip service) and they leave Islam like the arrow exits the kill.[17] And it has been reported in a *hadîth* that the similitude of the hypocrite who reads the Quran is that of sweet basil (*rayhân*), its smell is sweet but its taste is bitter. Based on the above, it is not inconceivable that one who learns the outward forms of knowledge may be a hypocrite and transgressor. His sign will be that he does not derive benefit or give benefit from the knowledge, rather, he harms himself and others too.

In summary, the scholar that acts upon his knowledge and teaches it is virtuous, benevolent and included among the heirs of the prophets. The scholar who does not embody his knowledge but teaches people knowledge and righteousness, his situation is precarious but he is better than the evil scholar who neither acts upon nor teaches the good he has learned, as a result he invites to wrongdoing by facilitating its means and opening up its doors. So distinguish between the scholars and follow the best of them, adopt his qualities, walk his path and you will be amongst those that are truly guided. Allah guides whom He wills to the straight path.

Know, may Allah have mercy on you, that the scholar who embodies his knowledge and is included amongst the scholars of the religion and the scholars of the Hereafter by Allah and His Messenger has signs and characteristics that distinguish him from the mixed up scholars described by Allah and His Messenger as the scholars of the tongue, followers of passion whose preference is for the temporal world rather than the Hereafter. Among the signs that distinguish him, is that he is humble, modest, fearful, and apprehensive through awe of Allah. He is a *zâhid*, that is, he is not attached to the temporal world and he is content with whatever little he possesses. He spends upon the righteous, gives counsel to the slaves of Allah and is compassionate and merciful towards them. He calls to good and prohibits evil. He is swift in performing good deeds and constant in worship. He directs towards good and invites towards guidance. His mark is reverence,

16   Related by Ahmed on the authority of Abû Dharr.
17   There are several narrations of this *hadîth*. Imam al-Nawawi and Ibn Hajar both comment that the meaning is that this type of person enters into and leaves Islam like the arrow enters and exits from the victim of the hunt, that is without gathering any of its flesh. There has been discussion of whether the meaning of the phrase 'leaves Islam' suggests they are out of the fold of the religion or whether the meaning of Islam is 'obedience' and that they are considered to be disobedient but within the fold. And Allah knows best.

tranquillity, deliberateness, good character, generosity, soft disposition and he lowers the wing of humility to the believers. He is not arrogant, haughty, covetous of people, desirous of the world and he prefers the Hereafter. He does not gather wealth or deprive others of their rights nor is he harsh or vicious. He is not bitter or argumentative nor does he prompt disputations. Neither is he stern or of bad character. He is not miserly or of the people of flattery and deceit nor does he give priority to the rich over the poor. He does not frequent the rulers nor is he silent towards them but is, within his capacity, critical of their wrongdoings. He does not desire status, wealth or position, rather he dislikes all of that and avoids involvement in any of it except where absolutely necessary and needed.

In summary, he is characterised by the praiseworthy traits and righteous acts that knowledge encourages and demands. He refrains from all the things that knowledge discourages such as blameworthy characteristics and actions. Every believer should adopt and adorn themselves with the qualities mentioned above. However, they are more important and more befitting for the scholar, in fact, they are obligatory upon him for he is a sign by which people are guided and a leader who is followed. If he goes astray and prefers the temporal world over the Hereafter then he is responsible for his sin and the sins of those that follow him. If he is upright and fearful of Allah, then he earns his reward and the reward of those who follow him.

It is necessary for the scholar to supplement the knowledge of external religious matters with inward characteristics related to the heart, the inner meanings (*asrâr*) of actions and the things that can destroy it (*al-afât*) and the knowledge of the divine threats (*wa'îd*) and promises (*wa'd*) mentioned in the Book and the Tradition (*sunnah*), such as the promise of reward for the righteous and punishment for the wrongdoers. By this, the scholar's benefit and his benefiting of others will be complete as the sacred sciences mentioned above are incomplete without each other. This is the knowledge of the righteous predecessors. One who reads their biographies will know that.

Inward knowledge has no foundation without knowledge of the outward while outward knowledge is incomplete without knowledge of the inward. As for knowledge of the divine promises and threats, they contain encouragement to the commandments and virtuous acts and dissuasion from the forbidden and vile acts. It is ugly for a scholar to speak of the rulings of compulsions or supererogatory acts except with mention of what has come to us from Allah and His Messenger. The chests of the believers are opened by the word of Allah, The Exalted, and His Messenger. By them, their hearts find peace and their aspirations rise.

Reflect upon this carefully and take a good amount from these three sciences. They are the science of the outward rules regarding worship and interaction, the science of the inward regarding the characteristics and matters pertaining to the heart and the science of the divine promise and threat, that is, what is mentioned by Allah and His Messenger on the merits of obedience, the *wa'd* and the threat of punishment for the wrongdoers, the *waîd*.

It is appropriate and well established that the people of knowledge should exceed in spreading their knowledge through their modesty and teaching. This is in reference to general knowledge of benefit to every single Muslim. The scholar's speech when mixing and sitting with the common folk should concern clarification of the obligations and prohibitions, supererogatory actions and obedience, reminders of the reward for goodness and punishment for wickedness, using a clear comprehensible style so that they can be aware and understand. He should not be silent, waiting for them to ask, when he knows they are in need or compelled to know something. For his knowledge of their need is itself a question implied by their state (*bi lisân al-hâl*).

The common folk desire leniency in religious matters regarding knowledge and actions. The scholars should not assist them in that by silencing their teaching and guidance. If they do that, destruction will prevail and tribulations will increase. When you test one of the common folk, and most people are common folk, you will find them ignorant of the obligations and prohibitions and matters of the religion about which ignorance is not permitted. If you do not find him totally ignorant, you will find him ignorant of some aspects and that if he does know something it is often from hearsay such that if you wished to replace it with ignorance you could do so easily with little effort due to his lack of foundation and authenticity in his learning.

The scholar should look at the student when he approaches him. If he is unoccupied and able to comprehend the sacred sciences he should instruct him to study books. If he is from the common folk and intends merely to acquire the obligatory knowledge, then he should be taught verbally in a manner he can comprehend. All the issues should be condensed and not made lengthy by the reading of books that will be difficult for him to comprehend and for which he may not have the time. He will not require more than that, as the requirements of the common folk in relation to knowledge is not much.

It is necessary for the scholars, especially those in positions of authority to admonish the Muslims when there is discord among them. He should instil fear through what has been related from Allah, the Exalted, and His Messenger in terms of the limitations and the warnings regarding false allegations and testimony and oaths and corrupt transactions such as usury and so forth. They should be reminded of the Islamic legal measures in reference to these matters and the severe punishments therein. This occurs when ignorance prevails with an increase in greed and lack of concern for religion. How many of the common Muslims when they hear of the prohibitions of lying, false oaths and testimony turn away from what they had determined to do due to their ignorance and lack of knowledge?

In summary, the scholars must ensure that they gather with people for knowledge and speak to them about it and clarify it to them. The scholar's discourse should be related to the issue for which he has been approached. For example, if someone approaches him regarding the contract of marriage, he should address them about the rights of women, the dowry, and payment of her expenses with kindness and about having a good relationship with her. Another example is the issue of business contracts. His discourse should concern witnesses, the sound and corrupt matters pertaining to trade and so forth.

By Allah! This kind of speech is better and worthier in social gatherings than delving into empty talk or talking about issues that they may not be interested in. The scholar should not engage himself with those that engross themselves in worldly affairs. He should not spend any of his time in matters other than establishing the religion. As we have mentioned earlier, the scholar should ensure that his gatherings and social interaction with common Muslims is filled with teaching, exhorting and reminding them. It has become particularly important in this time where most common folk are overwhelmed by heedlessness and ignorance and turning away from knowledge. If the people of knowledge assist them in this by not teaching nor reminding people, corruption will be victorious and harm will prevail. This is the consequence of the laxity of the common folk about the affairs of the religion and the scholars not teaching or making them aware. There is no strength or power other than by Allah.

One of the most important roles of the scholar is to teach people through action before speech. He should not command them with a good action except that he himself performs it and is concerned about it. He should not forbid them from a wrong action unless he refrains from it and is intense in his avoidance of it. He should only seek the Countenance of Allah and the Next World in his knowledge, his teaching and his action upon it and should wish for nothing else. The Messenger, upon him be peace, said, 'One who seeks knowledge that should be sought for Allah's sake so as to boast among the scholars and dispute with the foolish or to turn their attention towards him, will meet Allah and He will be angry with him'.

O Allah! Benefit us with what you have taught us, and teach us what will benefit us and increase us in knowledge. All praise is to Allah in every state. We seek refuge with Allah from the states of the people of the Fire.'